In Quest of the Least Coin

IN QUEST OF

THE LEAST COIN

By Grace Nies Fletcher
Illustrations by Lydia Rosier

WILLIAM MORROW & COMPANY, INC.

NEW YORK 1968

Foreword

THE MOST STEADYING STAFF in the hand of the modern Pilgrim progressing through today's Slough of Despond muddied by race riots and an undeclared bloody war of attrition is the Christian surety that life is more than a meaningless hodgepodge of violence and compassion, of pain and happiness, that God has a Plan for each man and woman. As a child needs love and security in the home, so man needs a hand to hold onto in the whirling vastness of the universe where his little spacecraft can so easily go "Poof!"

I like to think that my writing about the Fellowship of the Least Coin is a small part of the Plan, though I was a long time seeing the path leading to its next step forward. I first heard of the "new gifts of the widow's mite" when, in the spring of 1961, I met in New York City Felicia Sunderlal, the gentle Indian woman, graceful in her flowing sari, then Women's Secretary for Ecumenical Relations of the United Presbyterian Church, who was one of the ardent members of the international circle of prayer called The Fellowship of the Least Coin.

I wrote a few paragraphs of appreciation in my book *The Whole World's in His Hand,* and then flew back to the Orient to gather material for biographies of two outstanding women in Nepal and Japan. I came to know more and more intimately and to love these wise women of the East, educated by Christian missions, who are leading other women in their countries into proud international citizenship in the

5

Kingdom of God through their prayers, their example, and
their tiny symbolic gifts of the smallest coin in their countries. To discover what the Fellowship of the Least Coin is
quietly accomplishing in six continents around the world,
I visited ten countries where the women themselves explained to me how they were trying to help over some special
hump of despair or frustration the already established local
church, government, or interchurch projects. As independent
a traveler as I prefer to be, I can interpret this great experiment in the power of prayer only in terms of my own experience, of what I myself saw of their relief and educational
work for the needy of many faiths. The warmth of the welcome given me by fellow Christians, even when I could not
speak a word of their language nor they of mine, will linger
long in my memory. For we talked together in the language
of the heart and so were "strangely warmed."

If I were to thank all the kind and patient people who
have helped to make this person-to-person report possible,
the acknowledgments would run longer than the text. I
apologize in advance for all of importance I may have left
out, for the names of both people and places on the map
often spelled in two ways so that I had to choose one, willy-
nilly. Any unwitting discrepancies in detail will have to be
forgiven me, but I hope I have caught the *spirit* of the Fellowship of the Least Coin who share concern for every race
and creed.

GRACE NIES FLETCHER
October, 1967

Contents

In Quest of the Least Coin

One

Wise Women of the East

ONE BREATHLESSLY HOT MORNING in March, 1967, my interpreter and I drove far into the bush beyond Nairobi where the sun, new-minted, was scattering bright gold on the low hills. Everything about this shiny new democracy of Kenya (then only five years old) is a little more vivid than anywhere else—its impossibly blue sky; its red dirt roads, wounds in the green countryside; its valleys sparked by the fire of the flame trees; its eager people reaching passionately for an education for their children, for economic know-how, and for unity as a nation. This latter is made difficult by the inability of its many tribes to speak each other's language; but they all understand the great shout of *Uruhu—Freedom!* The Kikuyu women to whom I was scheduled to talk about the Fellowship of the Least Coin understood no English, and I could not say even "Thank you" or "Please" in Kikuyu. As the little red car bumped over the rough, unpaved road I wondered how even my fluent interpreter could translate us to each other, African to American. How could I make clear a world concept to women who had never seen a TV, to whom the radio was a voice from Olympus, and who could neither read nor write?

As I walked into the bare wooden hall set high upon a green hill, the atmosphere of intense excitement hit me like a slap in the face. Were the Kikuyus as uneasy as I was?

11

What was at first a blur of many colors separated itself into sixty-five women, each wearing her best shuka, her gay cotton dress, with a scarf to protect her head from the clouds of red dust and the blazing African sun. They were of all ages; old women, darkly inscrutable, with strands of gray, tightly curled hair peeping out from under the scarves; middle-aged women with hands horny from the panga (hoe); young mothers casually feeding from their bare breasts beautiful naked little black babies. Nearly all the audience were barefoot.

"Some have come twenty-five miles to hear you speak," my interpreter Mary Kirobi, the wife of an African Presbyterian minister who served seven village churches, murmured in my ear. Why? As I stood up to be introduced in a torrent of meaningless sounds, I worried, how could a stray American, jetting down from a cloud, speak significantly to these women to whom a rickety bus to rest their weary feet was the height of luxury? How could I paint realistically the world vision of an Indian woman of whom they had never heard, in a language they could not understand?

"I have come to tell you the story of Shanti Solomon, a woman from India who dreamed a dream," I said, and then I told them as simply as I could about the Fellowship of the Least Coin, begun by Asian women who had envisioned other women everywhere working constructively for peace, linking together all Christian women whatever their creed or nationality through prayer for each other. As a tiny symbol of their mutual concern, they gave each month the smallest coin of their country, be it baht, paisa, or penny, to help the sick, the poor, the despairing in Asia, Europe, Africa, and both Americas.

It was almost too hot to breathe. As I waited for the interpreter to translate, I watched the faces before me, shining with perspiration, still blank with the protective secrecy of the African. Now these people had political independence but little else. I had been in their smoke-blackened thatched huts with not even a chimney, where the only furniture was a three-legged stool and a couple of cooking pots. How could they possibly understand the merging of far horizons into a great circle of compassion?

Suddenly a woman in a bright red dress scattered with huge yellow daisies sprang to her feet, shouting something in Kikuyu. Startled, I asked the interpreter what she had said.

"She wants to know what *you* are getting out of this," the interpreter answered apologetically. "How much does the Fellowship of the Least Coin pay you?"

"Tell her, not a penny. I don't even belong . . . yet. I merely want to see with my own eyes what the members of the Fellowship who live in six continents are doing to help other women, children orphaned and hurt by war, hunger, or disease."

The woman in the red dress sat down, obviously not convinced I was telling the truth, while another older woman rose to ask, "Where are you going from here?"

"To Vietnam. To visit the refugees in the relief camps helped by Asian women."

"Don't you know there's a war on? It's dangerous!"

"So what? If nurses and doctors can go there, so can I. I'm not much good with a hypodermic but I can give pointed words for all the world to read."

The murmur that rippled across the hall was cut through by the shrill voice of the daisy woman, who had sprung again to her feet. But this time her dark face was shining, filled with light. She talked so fast the interpreter had trouble keeping up. This is what this bare-footed Kikuyu woman said:

"I want to go to Vietnam with you! I too have lived in government camps behind barbed wire [Mau Mau camps]. But there I became a Christian. That is why I'd like to tell them in Vietnam that light comes after dark. I am not a rich American; I cannot afford to go. *But I can go with you in my prayers for peace.* How do I join the Fellowship of the Least Coin?" I didn't know exactly how, but suggested they send on their request to their church's national headquarters.

Every single one of the sixty-five women in that crowded hall wanted to join too! The interpreter had to write down their names for them. Ngai, Wambui, Wangin, other names I could not even pronounce. But they were no longer strangers. As I left, one of these women put her warm dark cheek against mine in farewell and they all prayed for my safety on my "Grand Safari." Tears of wonder choked my throat. For Shanti Solomon had been right. All women, be they college graduates or illiterates, rich or poor, speak the same language of the heart.

Trying to put into words, either Kikuyu or English, how the women of the Fellowship of the Least Coin are helping in relief work for the sick, homeless, and downtrodden of six continents, is rather like describing a sunrise to a blind man—all one can do is to give the *feeling* of color and glory. As soon as I decided to tell this story of focusing the power of prayer in a practical way by a world fellowship of Christians, I realized I had to consult with the Wise Women of the East again before I tried to introduce them to anyone else, so I rushed to buy an airplane ticket to ten countries. At each airport, London, Nairobi, Delhi, Colombo, Singapore, Saigon, Bangkok, Manila, Hong Kong, and Tokyo, I was met by a hostess from the Fellowship who interpreted to me the peculiar genius of her own country and displayed the projects being helped by the tiny paisas, baht, centavos, yen, or pennies given by concerned Christian women in twenty-nine countries.

It was an amazing experience to find a doctor of theology washing diapers for retarded children in a Ceylonese river one day and the next to be riding with Asian relief workers in Vietnam upon a road where we had to look out for mines,

Vietcong, and water buffaloes! New groups in different countries were being added to the Fellowship so rapidly that
before a display could be set up showing where the women
were praying and what was being done in 91 villages, cities
or refugee camps, the map was already out of date. (Kenya
and Liberia joined while I was still hopping jets.) So I
decided that the only way to give even an inkling of how the
Fellowship were helping to meet emergencies of war, floods,
riots, plagues, and hunger was to select from each country
an example of a *different kind* of Christian missionary investment, whether it be research into a tribal culture in
order to make the gift significant or merely handing a tin
pail of milk to a small hungry child. The only thing all these
projects had in common was the prayer and the least coin
of her country by which the giver pledged her personal
concern.

"Just what is this Fellowship of the . . . what do you
call it? . . . where you give only twelve piddling pennies
a year for world relief?" demanded my American seatmate
skeptically as our V.C. 10 knifed through the clouds on our
way from London to Nairobi. "We have too many organizations already, church societies, CARE, United Fund . . ."

"The Fellowship of the Least Coin isn't another *organization;* it's a *movement* among Christian women regardless of
political or theological differences," I explained. "It sprang
up spontaneously in the Far East, in India and Manila, spread
through all Asia, then leaped the oceans to the West because
it answered the desperate query of women everywhere,
'What can I do as a Christian to stop war? To keep my
sons from dying on the battlefield? To substitute tolerance
and forgiveness for hate and guns?' The answer was 'Begin
in your home to practice and to teach your own children
how to forgive.' "

"I believe in that, too." My seatmate began to fumble in
her handbag, handed me a dollar, triumphantly. "Here!"

I gave her back the bill. "Thank you. *But money is not*

important. Or perhaps I should say it is important in a different way. For the first time in history the poor East can give back to help the wealthy West *on a proud, equal basis.* The poorest woman in an Indian village, giving each month her tiny paisa (about an eighth of an American penny) is no longer merely an object of charity. She gives on the same level as the woman in a New York penthouse. She asks God's blessing upon a woman in a country not her own and, as practical token of her sincerity, she sets aside her smallest coin for those in need wherever they may live."

The American considered a moment, then reached inside her coin purse to hand me a penny. I sighed and gave that back, also.

"If you really want to join the Fellowship, save it for your first month's sharing. No one knows for whom or where your penny will be spent, for the small coins go to all women everywhere and are given without fanfare. What is really urgent is not your money, but your prayers and your concern."

Thus simply, by word of mouth and sponsored nationally by church women of each country in their own chosen way, the Fellowship of the Least Coin has spread quietly around the world. The Fellowship seldom initiates projects but helps along those already in progress. Moreover it never announces how much money has been raised by any one country in order to prevent comparisons. The idea originated in the Far East, spread from Asia to the West. Pennies, francs, bahts, centavos, winged by prayer—"the widow's mite" that became mighty because along with her tiny coin, she gave herself.

Shanti Solomon, whose first name means "peace" and whose surname connotes "wisdom," is the splendid new woman of Asia, educated by Christian missions, who does not trot meekly behind her husband, carrying the bundles, but who stands proudly beside her man. These wise women of the East whose own ancestors may have been subject to

Moslem purdah or Hindu suttee, or considered mere chattels by their Buddhist husbands, understand as no Western woman possibly could the yearnings of the uneducated, desperate women whether in the African bush, in Vietnamese rice fields, or in our American country or city ghettos; women whose lives have no future except child bearing, unremitting physical toil, whose only certain rest is death. Meanwhile, the mother's chief problem is to get enough food for her family to have at least one good meal a day. Slowly but surely these educated women of Asia, second to none in intellect, poise, world vision, are lifting these innumerable toiling mothers to a new sense of their own identity and of their kinship with other women around the world.

To understand how much such fellowship can mean both to the woman who has nothing and to the woman who has everything, it is enlightening to unweave the strands of the life story of Shanti Solomon (as she told it to me), to watch how she grew from a timid wife living in a mud-walled home in an Indian village to her full stature as a world citizen.

Shanti, born in Sambhal, Uttar Pradesh, India, on June 10, 1920, is the daughter of Nanhe Mall, who was forty-seven when Shanti was born, the twelfth child of the family. Nanhe Mall grew up as a Hindu. His first affianced wife, only seven years old, died before she matured sufficiently to come to her husband's home. His second wife died in child birth, but Nanhe was luckier in the life span of his third wife, Lilzzie Singh, whom he married when she was fourteen. Only a child herself, she knew little about modern infant care so that only three of her twelve survived, one son, Johnson, Shanti, the baby, and her older sister, Helen.

Lilzzie Singh, however, had been born into a Christian family, although she never attended a mission school, since it was considered beneath the family dignity for her to associate with children of castes lower than her own Khatri, or warrior, caste. Accordingly the five girls of the Singh family were tutored by an Episcopalian priest. Shanti warns, "You must remember that in India the pride of caste dies hard, as does the concept of absolute obedience to your husband."

Shanti's father was murdered by his own Hindu family for becoming a Christian. When Nanhe Mall decided to be baptized he went all the way and became an evangelist. The Mall family, who were Banya merchant caste, were so outraged at this betrayal that they went to court to try to prevent his ever inheriting any part of his Hindu patrimony. To the credit of the Indian court, the family lost. There was only one thing to do, to take "justice" into their own hands.

"So they poisoned my father," Shanti relates matter-of-factly. "There was no secret about it; the whole village knew what had happened. It was not unheard-of for a family tribunal to condemn to death a member who had broken their sacred Hindu tradition. I was only six weeks old when my father died, but my mother has told me often what happened on that last day. Just before he died, my father came out of the coma into which he had lapsed, asked my mother to put me, wrapped in her shawl, in his arms. He spoke to me as if I could understand. 'I am leaving you fatherless, poor little girl, child of my love. The only heritage I can leave you is being a Christian. You will not want for anything, ever. You belong to the Lord's family. He will look after you.'

"And He did," Shanti says quietly. "He and my mother.

"Lilzzie Singh, although of a higher caste than her husband, yet obeyed him even in death. She kept my father's words alive for us children. He had always been the ruler in his own house; what he said my mother still did. She refused the shelter his Hindu family was forced by custom to offer us; instead she went to work herself as a teacher, and then as hostess in a hostel, an unheard-of thing for a high-caste Indian woman to do. But being a widow in a Hindu family is almost to die yourself or to become a vegetable with no voice of your own. At thirty-three my mother further defied public opinion by becoming a Bible woman in our village. Not overly strong in body, working long hours for little pay, she nevertheless ran a gay and happy home; she taught us three children how satisfying it is to stand on your own two feet.

"Often there wasn't quite enough to eat and seldom meat to fold into our chapattis, but we learned early to share what we had. Sometimes my Grandmother Singh came to stay with us children while my mother worked, even though Grandmother was so frail that her head shook all the time. When some gift came to us, fruit, perhaps a chicken leg or goat meat, my mother would tell us children, 'Give it to your grandmother, for she is older.' My brother, Johnson Mall, who was only four, mischievous and hungry, would say, 'No, give it to me! Grandmother does not want anything to eat. See, she is shaking her head!' "

When Shanti smiles, the tiny wrinkles around her eyes smooth out and she is young again, remembering how her mother used to call her, "Shanti, my peace." "I guess I was spoiled," she admits. "Johnson now has three children of his own and is registrar at the famous Ludhiana Medical College. My sister taught in the government school before she retired; we now live together at Etawah, a town on the main railroad line between Calcutta and Delhi. The success of our family in finding satisfying jobs is due to my mother's courage in buckling on the armor of faith, both in God and in herself."

Shanti today is a small, gentle woman with infinite compassion in her dark eyes. She has known hunger, deathly fatigue, injustice in the murder of her father and despair at watching, helpless, for two years while her husband, Reuben Solomon, slowly died. But she has also two college degrees, has been around the world several times and has been welcomed by many nations as the representative of her great country, free India. Yet she is strangely humble. She has little money but never worries about tomorrow. Once she went around the world with only the sixty rupees (five dollars) for spending money which India allows her citizens to take out of the country. When she shopped for saris recently to wear to the United States as the speaker at important conferences ranging from California to New York, she told the clerk in the Delhi store, "No silk, please. Just cotton."

But she has been rich in the devotion of both her mother and her husband. Shanti and Reuben Solomon fell in love, drawn together by their common interest in education. After her graduation from Isabella Thoburn College where Reuben's half sister, Dr. Eva Shipstone, is now principal, Shanti taught English and geography for ten years in various Indian schools before she and Reuben were married at Budaun, UP, in 1950. The son of a Methodist minister, he was professor of history and psychology in a Hindu college. Higher education is a status symbol in India, so their wedding was an important social affair to which even her father's estranged family came, bearing gifts.

For once Shanti, as a bride, was regal in white Benares silk shot with silver, her sari edged with heavy silver embroidery. She wore no veil but the usual gold ornament on her forehead with the golden chain gilding the part in the soft dark hair. Their wedding gifts set them up in housekeeping and added to their modest savings—bangles and bracelets of heavy gold from her Hindu relatives; brass kitchen utensils, but none of iron, for those were bad luck; three plated silver tea sets for her to polish; great quantities of household linen and other thoughtful donations from her Christian relatives.

"A wedding in India, even a Christian one, is very expensive, for it involves the whole community," Shanti explains. "We invited as special guests only our families and close friends, including the minister who married us. But the whole congregation of the Methodist church which we attended and all the neighbors came in afterward to celebrate and incidentally to be fed. But that is not the end." Shanti smiles ruefully. "When the giver of your wedding present has a marriage in his family, you are supposed to give back to the new bride and groom a little more than you received."

"So Reuben and I were soon as poor as usual." Shanti chuckles. "But that did not matter, any more than my being an old maid. Imagine an Indian bride of thirty! But by then I knew my own mind. Reuben was passionately Indian in spite of his English name, which he was given at baptism as were many others because this gave him preference in getting jobs under the British. But Reuben was especially broad-minded about me as his wife; although he would not let me work any longer for money as long as he had a salary (he was presently employed in a "model village" project under the Ford Foundation), he allowed me to give voluntary help to the village women and to the church. When women's committees met in Delhi or some other place far away, I did not want to leave Reuben alone, but he would push me out. 'Go, Shanti,' he would urge. 'You will become a bigger person.'"

Another American village worker who visited them during their honeymoon days recalls:

"I remember the first time I visited Shanti in their village home about ten miles from the Agricultural Institute, Alahabad. Their home was a 'model' house which with very little more investment than the usual, could be duplicated in any village. It had mud walls three feet thick; even then the white ants came through and were a pest. She cooked on a model 'smokeless chulha' (stove) and her house and kitchen were open at all hours for whoever came to see and, it was hoped, learn. Because of the presence of a 'foreigner' such visits began early when I was there. The morning tea was prepared under questioning about the chulha, the content of the meal, why it was served to the three of us together (in India men usually eat before the women, but we three—Shanti, Reuben and I—ate together). The washing up of the dishes brought more questions. So it was throughout the day. I felt as though I were living in Grand Central Station, but Shanti maintained a quiet serenity. She patiently answered all questions, even though the same ones were asked by five different people in succession. When I asked her how she stood it—two days had been enough for me—she replied, 'It's a bit worse because you are here, but I don't mind it. It gives me a chance to explain and if they hear it often enough, they'll learn.'

"She had a pile of poster teaching aids for child care, personal hygiene, charts for learning how to read, instructions for sewing and knitting clothes for a family. If a child got sick, she would take him with his mother to the local hospital, stand by to interpret what the doctor prescribed in everyday words the mother could understand. Thus she helped overcome the villagers' fear of foreign medicine.

"She utilized every opportunity to teach by example.

"I remember we were going into the fields one day and Shanti took up a small hand-trowel. She said, 'I must carry this because so many of the women think I go to the fields for "necessity" as they do and right now we are trying to teach them to bury all such refuse.' She didn't need to do it; she had a small bucket-flushed latrine in the courtyard of the house, but she did it to identify herself with the women amongst whom she lived."

Shanti did not preach with words but if the villagers asked her why she and her husband were helping them in their community projects, she would say simply, "Because we are followers of Jesus Christ." If they wanted to know more, she told them. When there was bitter warfare between Moslems and Hindus in India, Shanti went to terrified victims on both sides to ask, "What can I do to help *you?*" This early she had the belief that religious differences do not necessarily result in hate but may be resolved by love.

In 1956, the Presbyterian Church, concerned because bitterness still existed between those countries which had been on opposite sides of World War II, organized an International Fellowship Team of Reconciliation, six church women who were to go to Alaska, Japan, Korea, Hong Kong, and the Philippines to try to knit together the raveled sleeve of Christian forgiveness. Shanti Solomon was asked to go from India; the other team members included a Japanese, Miss Taruko Ohashi, and four Americans, Mrs. R. G. Carl, Mrs. James Wiltsie, Miss Margaret Shannon, and Mrs. A. H. Lang from Alaska.

Shanti, who had seldom gone alone even to market and who certainly had never ridden in a train without some other woman with her, was terrified of leaving her own familiar country, let alone flying across dark unknown oceans in her first plane ride to the home of the polar bears and the bitter cold! Besides, although she had no children to worry about, how could she leave Reuben to manage for himself for three long months?

"But he pushed me out into my great adventure." Pride makes a deep note in her melodious Indian voice. (Why is it that the voices of executive women in the West are so frequently strident?) " 'Of course you must go,' he said. 'It is a great opportunity to see how the rest of the world lives and thinks, to bring back new concepts to our village women —and to me.' "

Reuben went to the airport in Delhi to see her off. Their eyes were fastened on each other as they faced their first long separation. Indians do not weep in public nor show the panic Shanti felt when they stood together under the shadow of the great silver wings that were to bear her away from her husband. He walked beside her to the plane's gangway, urging, "Shanti, you must go now." Did he have some inner premonition, vague but real, that the great vision Shanti was to bring back to India would be her own? That behind the locked doors of her present understanding

lay the concept of the world Fellowship of the Least Coin?
Probably not.

The Pacific Team gathered first in Tokyo, where together
they planned their continuing trip. But the postwar bitterness dismayed them, for both Shanti and the Japanese team
member had been refused admittance into Korea. Shanti
had protested, puzzled, "But India is neutral. We believe in
nonviolence. What can Korea have against me?" The reasons
were political, had nothing to do with her personally, she
was assured.

One American cried impulsively, "If you and Teruko
can't go, the rest of us will not go either! What is the use?
Our whole purpose of reconciliation is defeated already."

"No, go along," Shanti urged. "I want to ponder this
matter in my heart. I shall wait for you in Manila with our
Christian friends there, studying to see if perhaps I myself
have wrong thoughts."

She still had a prickle of conscience, wondering what this
setback had to do with her, what she personally could do to
foster better relations. She told herself, "The wounds of
Hiroshima and Nagasaki are still raw; that I can understand.
But the Americans, too, lost many sons. They came here not
as conquerors, but humble, putting their Christian concern
higher than national pride. It is easier to sympathize with
the underdog but the overdog needs kindness, too. As an
Indian, I can see both sides."

The Team had invited two new Asian members, Mrs.
Rayann Ma of Hong Kong and Mrs. Carmen Armonio of the
Philippines, to go with them to Korea to replace the Japanese
and the Indian. As Shanti searched her Bible with her
friends in Manila, she found the answer she was looking for
in the story of the Good Samaritan who succored the man
who fell among thieves. She saw, "We village women in
India have drawn away our skirts from the terrible suffering
of the war-torn mothers and children, everywhere. We have
been like the priest who passed by on the other side, saying

smugly, 'This is not my business!' What can I do *now* to bring together all these women who have been so badly bent?"

She was still pondering while she and the group of women in the Manila church read together the gospel of Mark. When they reached the twelfth chapter where Jesus comments that the widow who gave her two infinitesimal coins had given more than any other because she had given all she had, Shanti's heart gave a great leap.

"The widow's mite! That's the answer!" Shanti cried aloud as the Filipinos looked up at her, startled. Her dark eyes shone, her lips trembled with eagerness to make them understand. "You have to give *yourself* along with your least coin. Real giving is a throwing off of pride. Only when our hearts are empty of self can God fill them with love and forgiveness. Why could we not start a fellowship where all women, any woman, shall pray for another in a different land? There must be some concrete symbol of her concern —possibly the smallest coin of her country? Like the widow's mite, to help people sick, in bad trouble everywhere? What do you think? Could we do this?"

"It is a great plan! I'm for it!" One enthusiastic Filipino lady, Mrs. Maria Tadiar, came up to throw her arms around the trembling, excited Indian dreaming of a great peace, of women holding the world in their folded hands.

"You can't see a prayer or an atom, but both can have great power for good," Shanti rushed on. "If women all over the world taught understanding of each other in their homes to their children, who knows what might happen? To release this power may take time, but what other practical way is there to prevent war? The one small coin we save every month, wouldn't amount to much but it would be a beginning."

When the Filipino women enthusiastically agreed, Shanti recalls, "I got a warm feeling in my heart."

But when the rest of the Team met Shanti again in Manila,

one American said skeptically, "I do not think our church women would want to be bothered with saving only twelve pennies every year!"

"That's what's wrong with you who have everything," Shanti pointed out, patiently. "You don't understand how humiliating it is to always be on the receiving end as we are in Asia! The paisa, the least coin of my country, is worth only a fraction of an American penny, but even the poorest village woman can afford to give it to someone worse off than she is. She needs to do it *for her own sake!* To stand up proudly. It is important that rich and poor, college graduate and illiterate, *can give on the same level.* If you of the West draw aside your skirts, you'll be the loneliest women in the world. Your great money has divided us; let's see if your least coins can draw us together!" They agreed heartily. When the invitation was later extended to other Christian women in the United States, South America, Europe and Africa, they gladly joined the Fellowship of the Least Coin first sparked in Manila.

Back again in Tokyo, Shanti, invited to speak to a church gathering, could hardly wait to tell the Japanese women about the new plan of her heart. The entire Team prayed before she left for the meeting that she be given the right words to make the Japanese understand the power of forgiveness to wipe out bitterness. However, Shanti found that the women gathered together to meet her had arranged to discuss the innocuous question, "why Jesus had cursed the poor little fig tree so that it died."

Shanti said gently, "I know how you Japanese love trees, cherry blossoms and Mount Fuji. But before you get too concerned about the poor little fig tree, ask yourselves which are more important, trees or people? Are not both known by their fruits? In India, my home, the Hindus are most respectful of all living things, monkeys, cows, peacocks, even bugs. Some people wear masks lest they unwittingly breathe in or hurt a flea! But the Hindu is not taught to love his enemy. My father was a Hindu before he became a Christian; he used to say, 'The Hindu believes, "If someone hurts me, I must pay him back in his own coin." But the Christian says, "I must go a step beyond; I must forgive him." '

"Then I told the Japanese women about the Fellowship of the Least Coin which helps not only the recipient but the giver, but they were not yet ready to receive it."

But Shanti, having planted the seed, knew it did small good to dig it up like a child to see why it was not growing faster. It was two years before the first group of Japanese women joined the Fellowship of the Least Coin, but today, there is scarcely a women's group in the Kyodan, the United Church of Japan, who do not give their prayers and their yen each month for relief work in many nations. No giver ever knows where her small coins will be spent, for they are sent to the treasurer of the World Council of Churches to be assigned to many nations by the women of the East Asia Christian Conference who act as stewards. Although the money raised in a country is never returned there directly but is put into the world fund for distribution, the Asian women respond to requests for help from all continents. Their interest extends from helping to build a chapel on the Chiba peninsula at the mouth of Tokyo Bay for use by the former prostitutes in the Rehabilitation Colony, many of whom have become blind, feeble-minded or paralyzed (the Cross on this chapel is visible to every ship that sails to Tokyo) to caring for blind children in the Helen Keller Home in Jerusalem and for similar blind youngsters in New York City, as well as for crippled children from all over Kenya. They help to educate children and young people in Colombia, South America, in the Philippines, in Paris, France, and in East Germany. They send swift emergency relief to Thailand, Vietnam, India, and Pakistan. They do not inundate with oceans of cash but drop the gentle rain of their love and understanding upon parched people in many lands. Shanti marvels, "One never knows where compassion may be carried by the divine wind which bloweth where it listeth."

The idea of praying and giving, person to person, on an equal basis in both East and West, has swept like wildfire around the world. Women in seven countries that first year began saving their tiny coins in as many kinds of receptacles as there were nations. In Malaya, the women used as piggy banks short sticks of bamboo in whose hollow center they were accustomed to hide their family savings. In Pakistan and India, where the family treasure among villagers used to be put into earthen pots, buried in the ground, the women made little brown clay pots; some village women even stuck the pots to the mud wall of their homes so they would not forget to put in their monthly paisa, a fraction of a rupee. In the United States, the Presbyterians, who fostered the Fellowship, prepared small cards with a place for each of the twelve pennies, below the picture of a woman in another country for whom the giver could pray, including women in Guatemala, India, the United States, the Philippines, Brazil, Iran, Pakistan, Thailand, Portugal and Colombia.

"This must not be just another organization with monthly meetings and a deadly dull secretary's report," Shanti insisted. "The Fellowship is a spontaneous sharing by women everywhere in the power of the spirit which may be turned to a given end as surely as sunlight focused by glass upon a bit of wood may burn. The small coins should not interfere with either local or other church giving, for they are only symbols." But by the end of the first year, the Asian women were startled to find that these coins, some so valueless that when a person dropped one she did not stoop to pick it up, amounted to $11,000. Next year it totaled over $20,000. The tiny coins continued to accumulate till they amounted to $100,000.

"What shall we do with all this money? How shall we distribute it?" These questions were asked by the women who gathered for the first Asian Church Women's Conference held in Hong Kong in 1958. Since their churches were all members of the recently organized East Asia Christian Conference, it was agreed that this organization should administer the funds. (This conference with headquarters in Bangkok includes in its membership churches extending from Korea on the north, south to Australia and New Zealand, west to Pakistan and as far east as Japan.) The women formed a Central Committee to interpret and promote the Fellowship of the Least Coin, to receive applications for grants and to make recommendations to the all-Asia Conference as to where the funds from the Least Coins should be spent.

Little did they dream that within ten years this money would amount to over half a million dollars!

At the Third Asian Christian Women's Conference held in 1966 in Tokyo with the Japanese Church women as hostesses, the tenth anniversary of the Fellowship's founding was celebrated, Shanti was given a bracelet made from tiny coins collected around the world, and Chairman Jannuan Suriyakham, from Thailand, summed up two important aspects of the Fellowship as follows:

(1) In interpreting the Least Coin, we strongly stress the following principles:
   (a) The fact that not more than the least coin in our currency be given to this fund in order to keep the idea that every woman can give the same amount to this project. (It should not be in competition with the regular church giving.)
   (b) That the covenant of prayer and world fellowship be emphasized, rather than the form of raising the money or the amount.
(2) In administering the funds, the following should be some guiding principles:
   (a) Since it is true that countries beyond Asia are contributing to the Least Coin, it is necessary that all the money should not be spent in Asia.

(b) That the major part of the money be spent on Evangelism and Relief Work.

(c) That some of the money be reserved for ventures of international fellowship among women or to send women delegates to ecumenical meetings.

(d) That projects may be proposed by women's organizations which participate in the Fellowship of the Least Coin.

It is a great joy to know that the gifts we have shared have helped the hungry, the destitute, and those in need around the world. We believe that this Christian giving and service supported by the chain of prayer will help bring the world peace.

The decision that individual women might join the Fellowship of the Least Coin, even if their home churches did not foster the movement, opened the door of participation for Roman Catholics, for women from Methodists to Mormons.

Today the Fellowship of the Least Coin has contributing members or has given aid in twenty-nine countries, including Australia, Brazil, Burma, Cameroon, Ceylon, Chile, Colombia, Guatemala, Hong Kong, India, Indonesia, Iran, Japan, Korea, Lebanon, Liberia, Mexico, New Zealand, Pakistan, the Philippines, Portugal, Scotland, Syria, Taiwan, Thailand, the United States, Vietnam, Venezuela, and Yugoslavia. The Fellowship goes on and on quietly, with its comparatively small gifts, forging little links of understanding and reconciliation between one nation and another, weaving the hopeful fabric of peace.

The Fellowship's grants to the United States have included tutoring school children from substandard homes and training former adolescent drug addicts in the East Harlem Protestant Parish for jobs, and financing a similar project in a church in Greenwich Village; craft training for unskilled workers in the Delta Ministry in Mississippi, which is trying to find food and employment for desperate share-croppers pushed out of their dilapidated homes; schools for migrant workers; and, this past year, Braille Bibles for our blind children. Asia, Europe, Africa and South America helping the richest country in the world to solve her problems!

These praying women have even nonchalantly pushed aside the Iron Curtain to encourage students in East Berlin and Czechoslovakia; Yugoslavia both gives and receives the help of the Least Coins. Where money cannot be sent out of the country, arrangements have been made to credit the amount raised to their account by the treasurer of World Council of Churches at Geneva. However, even the wise women of the East were surprised when Buddhist and Moslem women applied for membership in this Christian women's movement! I sat at a table with a group of these leaders in Manila recently when the request came in. After catching a breath, these world-minded Asians answered, reasonably, "Why not? You pray to the same God and if you want to help in Christlike giving to the needy of all nations, welcome!" After all, how can one foster "the peaceable kingdom" unless she exhibits equal tolerance herself?

Long-time peace may well turn out to be a woman's job, weaving together the strong nylon rope of mutual compassion in quiet homes all over the globe.

"The men haven't done such a good job with their bombs and bullets," remarked one Chinese mother ruefully, who is trying to raise eight children in uneasy Hong Kong. "Perhaps these have been necessary to keep us free. *But wars do not stay won without putting yourself into the other fellow's shoes . . . without daily sacrifice.* We women can teach our sons and daughters that the Kingdom of Heaven does not stop at the Seventeenth Parallel nor at the Iron or Bamboo Curtain; that all men are brothers in the family of God. We mothers have *got* to get together, for when our sons die on the battlefield, a little of us dies, too."

Two

The Fellowship of the Least Coin Comes to East Harlem

> *From the beginning of its ministry, the East Har-*
> *lem Protestant Parish has been supported by the*
> *gifts and prayers of fellow Christians. No gift has*
> *ever brought such encouragement and a deep sense*
> *of the unity of the church to our staff and mem-*
> *bers as the gifts from the Fellowship of the Least*
> *Coin. In many ways, the value of the gift has thus*
> *gone far beyond the child care program for which*
> *it was appropriated . . . and has lifted our eyes*
> *beyond East Harlem.*
>
> LETTY RUSSELL, *staff member, New York City*

IN THE WALLED CITY of Hong Kong I had seen babies under two years old confined alone all day in a sort of chicken coop because their mother had to leave them to work on the road. I had stepped gingerly over piles of refuse and open sewers in Kathmandu, Nepal. But East Harlem toward which my taxi was now rattling was different because it was my own; it belonged to me and I was partly responsible for it if only because it was to me an equally foreign city. I expected to find there crumbling buildings, rats, garbage, poor schools, adolescent gangs and drug addicts; they were all there cer-

tainly, but what I was unprepared for was the stirring of a
new spiritual rebirth, the pride of many neighbors working
and planning together to make this city within a city a
better place to be. In short, to thousands East Harlem was
home.

East Harlem Protestant Parish is an integral part of this
neighborhood of 185,000 people crowded into a district of
New York City that runs roughly from East 96th Street north
to 125th Street and east from Fifth Avenue to the Harlem
River. Its ministers and their families not only work but live
there, as do the lay members of the staff. This unique inter-
denominational Parish was started in 1948 by the Methodists, American Baptists, Congregational Christians, and
Presbyterians to devise new methods by which the church
could "come alive" in a community where only twenty percent of the people ever darkened a church door and those
few usually to be married or buried. In fact, there was no
church of a major denomination for them to go to if they
wished. There are now six denominations represented in the
Parish staff including, besides the original members, the
Evangelical and Reformed Church and the Evangelical
United Brethren. They first started to work in storefronts to
be nearer the people and even twenty years later they support only two large conventional church buildings, for, in
their philosophy, bricks do not make a church but loving
your neighbor does. Their only creed is to "live Christ" in
a mixed neighborhood which is forty percent Negroes, forty
percent Puerto Ricans, many of whom speak little English,
and a sprinkling of Italians and other early immigrants.

One of the lay staff of the Parish warned me subtly against
making snap judgments about what I saw there by telling me
about Joey, her small brother who had gone from his 101st
Street home to summer camp in Connecticut. There he saw
for the first time grass you could step on, wild flowers you
could pick, and his small fellow campers dancing around the
fire of an evening, shouting, "Wah hoo! I'm heap big Sioux!"

She ended, "The first postcard Joey sent home to us read: 'Funny thing. Everybody here is Indians!'"

The great majority of the East Harlem dwellers are not Indians, criminals, nor drug addicts; they are parents and children who want to get ahead economically and socially but don't quite know how to go about it. My taxi driver, friendly, inquisitive, and loquacious, soon found out that I was alone, a stranger in his city, so when I gave him the address I wanted on East 103rd Street, he protested, "But, lady, you don't want to go there. That's where them junkies are!"

"That's why I'm going, to meet them at Exodus House," I explained. "I'm writing a book."

"Oh, well then . . ." Naturally all authors were a little touched in the head. Why couldn't I write about the Pan Am building? Or the Art Museum? Something nice, now? But in spite of his muttered disapproval, he drove me to the address which I wanted, but it proved to be only a very large hole in the ground. I stared blankly beyond the broken sidewalk edged with overflowing refuse barrels, spewing out empty tin cans and garbage. On the other side of the littered street was a blank-looking building with darkly shuttered windows and with a padlock and chain across the heavy door, beside which was a small sign, *Exodus*.

"I ain't gonna leave here till I see you safe inside them locks," the taxi driver insisted as I climbed out of his cab. There was no bell visible but as I pounded upon the door, a man's voice drawled behind me, "I'm goin' in there, too, lady." The wind blew dirty newspapers about my ankles while the tall black friendly man produced a key from his dungarees. The door opened. I could hear the gears of the taxi, still protesting, clash and drive away.

Inside the Exodus office was warmth from the bitter March wind and cheerful electric light. An attractive girl sat at the telephone switchboard and a stenographer at her desk, while at a bare wooden table a man was busily writing down the names of a group of adolescent boys and slightly older men.

How could you tell an addict? One boy about sixteen glanced over at me with a glazed, lost look in his eyes with dilated pupils, yawned widely, and suddenly I knew.

"Eleven hundred junkies a year go in and out our door; maybe a quarter of 'em we can help," my new friend went on. "I'm an ex-addict myself. So I know horse [heroin] isn't any cure for what's wrong inside you; it's only a crutch, to help because you're scared . . . scared that you'll never get to *be somebody*. That's why group therapy in hospitals and prisons helps. But when the kid gets out on his own is when he most needs a friend; maybe he can go it alone but most likely not. It's the lonesomeness that gets you. You don't belong to a gang any more. Maybe your own family don't want you. Families can get put out of public housing if anyone there has pot in his possession. The pusher says, 'Glad to see you! Here, I'll give you a bag to celebrate!' There's free horse in that cellophane bag but the 'cured' kid knows if he gets hooked again, he'll have to pay $5 for the next fix. He comes to Exodus in a panic. So he meets some ex-addicts like me who've been through the mill, who'll go all the way with the kid when the goin' gets tough."

"Like Alcoholics Anonymous?"

"Sure. Only nobody here is anonymous." He glanced at the group around the worker busily signing them up. "And we're tough. If we take the junkie on, we run a urinalysis test six times a week to prove he means business. *He's got to admit he's been sick.* He's got to do that on his own or not even group therapy can help him. You wanna talk to our head man? He can tell you better'n me."

As I sat down at the businesslike desk of the director of Exodus, he answered my questions with a brisk report about "rehabilitation of the individual to his environment," "relating," and other professional shibboleths. I asked him, perhaps rudely, "Talk plain English, please. Why does a boy in East Harlem go on drugs, in the first place?"

The director explained, "In plain words, because of nothing to do but to hang around the street corner, because of despair of ever getting a decent job. Or maybe there are family problems, emotional insecurity. Some fool mother gives her son everything as far as she can but there's a hook on the end of it; he has to be her baby, do what she says. He finds he can't live up to what she expects of him; he wants some way to feel big. Heroin does this for him, takes him out of himself for a few rosy hours. Maybe his family doesn't even know the kid's a junkie till he's arrested for having drugs; then mama comes crying to us to help him. We do, but not the way she wants. We don't try to get her baby boy out of jail or the hospital; we know he's in a tough spot physically, mentally and emotionally, needs the doctor. But we send some ex-addicts to help with group therapy and when the patient gets out, these men stand by him. Sometimes we invite his family, too, to hear what goes on at the group sessions; so they can understand his problem.

"We train the kid for a job, car mechanic maybe, cabinet work, printing, things like that. We have forty ex-addicts in our workshops right now."

"Is that big hole across the street to be a new building?"

The director nodded. "Recently released patients need time to get adjusted to being outside, to be with people who understand what he's gone through. Our biggest job is to get him to *believe in himself.* Our tutors may even have to teach him to read and write."

"But surely our New York City children learn that much in public school!"

"You'd be surprised at the number of intelligent illiterates. Perhaps some teacher, badly trained herself, has told the boy he's too stupid to learn and he believes her, though he may have an IQ of 130! Our school children here in East Harlem test two years behind the students in, say, Westchester or Jersey suburbs with better social and economic backgrounds. We have a fifty percent *teacher* drop-out in Harlem every year. But once they discover that they really can learn, the ex-addicts rarely lapse. In a way, they're better off than the youngster now going to school because they have proved to themselves that they can lick the worst life can throw at them."

Exodus House is only one of the many community projects that the East Harlem Protestant Parish has started and later urged to take over its own management. "The Latin for 'project' means 'to throw,'" one staff member explained. "So when any group wants to manage on its own, we are delighted. We're like an amoeba. A bit breaks off, such as Exodus House, which is now incorporated though some of our staff are still on the board of managers. We like projects taking over control. It means the Parish is still alive and growing."

East Harlem has been described as "a rent jungle . . . where tenants are afraid to put out their lights at night for fear of rats." I saw there also the well advertised decaying walls wet from bad plumbing, floors where cockroaches crunched underfoot, filthy hallways with broken windows through which the bitter wind howled. But knock on a door and out into that icy corridor may come a couple of smiling, immaculately clean children whose tenement families obviously care for them the best they can. One staff member from the Parish admonished me sharply that to call East Harlem a jungle "sticks in the craw of everyone around here. Some have made it their home by choice rather than by necessity. To be sure there are danger, risks, and monumental problems which face people who live here, in which we participate, which in many ways victimize us. But the word 'jungle' and its overtones is, we believe, not a helpful one. It continues to stereotype this neighborhood with the kind of negative, dehumanizing connotations which white America thrives upon and which only confirms its prejudices as well as provides it with reinforcements to 'contain' the ghetto and to continue its isolation."

The Parish does not consider itself as made up of all "the

good guys" and all the rest of the world "the bad guys," he continued. "This sounds as if we are on the shore of a swirling river throwing life rings to drowning men. But as D. T. Niles [of East Asia Christian Conference, where the Least Coin Fellowship has its headquarters] points out, we are all drowning men—especially in a city which has such fantastic wealth, most of it 'white.' So, the beginning of self-understanding comes at the point where we are all in the swirling river together, and the church's function is to point a way to shore."

Fighting the loneliness of the big city where neighbors may not even understand each other's language, where the knock on the door may be a bill collector or a policeman, is one of the jobs of this kind of "live-in" church. The East Harlem Protestant Parish members have at their front doors a seal which reads: WELCOME IN THE NAME OF CHRIST. Below the clasped friendly hands and the Cross the invitation is repeated in Spanish, BIENVENIDO EN EL NOMBRE CHRISTO. One member translated this as, "Come in, friend, and stay a while."

When I was invited into one such apartment in a public housing building, the mother of five children had stripped all their beds, was doing her huge washing in an electric machine. She confessed over a hospitable cup of coffee, "The one thing I worry about—and from what I read, this is true out in the suburbs, too—is that one of my kids should get hooked on drugs. One of my son's high school friends, almost hysterical, called me one night to say he'd taken too big a dose of heroin. He was dangerously sick. What could I do? His family wouldn't call the police ambulance for fear of losing their apartment!" Her face lighted up. "But we're lucky. My oldest son's got a scholarship for next fall at Rutgers!"

Since education is the surest way of "getting to be someone," which solves many adolescent emotional problems, the East Harlem staff, whose headquarters is still in a converted store on Second Avenue, has taken part in Freedom Marches to get a new public school, and most of them have been in jail for thus standing side by side with their neighbors. To prevent dropouts if possible, individual tutorial help is also given to school children with special health or home problems, with a teacher for each pupil. One of the latest and most ambitious experiments is trying to get those who do graduate from high school into college.

I was invited to Sunday lunch by a young college graduate, a high school teacher who, after she finishes her own classes, is tutoring "high-risk" students. This is social service lingo for boys and girls whose grades are from 75 to 85%, too low for them to get into a Grade A college, but who have the intelligence potential to learn. Most of the staff families live in public housing, but my new friend and I toiled up five flights of dirty tenement stairs, ignoring the black scrawls on the walls. She opened her door into a charming apartment with sun-catching orange curtains, soft rugs on the polished parquet floor, and walls brightened by row upon row of many-colored book jackets. But there were bars at the front windows and—"What's that thing for?" I asked as I stumbled over a queer contraption, a two-foot iron bar that slid along a metal groove in the floor in front of the outer door.

"A police lock," the young teacher explained. "You know how frantic junkies are when they need cash. Even this lock was half-open one night when I came home late after tutoring. The police said that was all that saved me from being cleaned out."

I shivered. "Aren't you scared sometimes, living here alone?"

"I'd be lying if I said I wasn't," she admitted frankly. "But it's worth it. Antioch College is trying out some of the youngsters I sent to them and they're making good. This year I even got one girl into Wooster College in Ohio where I graduated!"

You'd think she had borne them, all these eager children

of whom she was so proud. One by one, little by little, looking toward the long tomorrow, Shanti Solomon and this American girl were saying the same thing: "This may not amount to much, but it's a beginning. . . ."

Ramon Diaz of the Parish staff described himself modestly as "a guy who loves kids," but *Harper's* Magazine has called him the sponsor of "The Gang Who Went Good." *

Ramon is an American from Puerto Rico who fought in the Korean War, stopped by East Harlem twenty years ago to call on his sister . . . and is still there. He was appalled by the teenager boy and girl gangs who roamed the streets, fighting, brawling, molesting pedestrians and sometimes even killing each other. "This is another kind of war," he told himself, worried. "Frightened, unhappy kids battling against poor schools, racial discrimination, dirt and poverty, and themselves. What can I do?"

"The Enchanters" was the name of one of the biggest gangs. They hung around a candy store run by La Viela, an old Puerto Rican woman who sold them reefers but who also kept a cigar box on the counter where a boy, temporarily penniless, could borrow, later pay the money back. The borrower always repaid or the gang roughed him up. They weren't worse essentially than any other adolescents; they just had nothing to do except fighting and indulging in drugs and sex. They needed a decent place of their own to go to. With ten people in a room at home, where could boys and girls meet except on sidewalks, in hallways or on roofs which were already crowded with adults also looking for privacy? Ramon was no trained social worker, but he was an American soldier; he had fought to give just such kids a chance.

"One of the big shots in the Enchanters gang sidled up to me one day," Ramon said, telling me his own story of what had happened. "He said, 'We wanna go social, Ramon. Will you tell us how?'"

* *Harper's* Magazine, June 1958, article by Dan Wakefield.

" 'You're kiddin',' I told him.

" 'On the level,' he insisted. 'What do we do?'

" 'First, you gotta gather up all the guns, pistols, rifles, knives, chains from the gang,' I told the kid.

" 'What for?' he asked, suspicious.

" 'We throw 'em into the East River,' I told him flat. 'You don't think anyone'll believe you've gone social with full battle equipment, do you?'

" 'No, I guess not!' the Enchanters' leader agreed. 'But what if the other gangs think we've gone chicken? We'd need a safe place to meet.'

" 'You'll have it,' I promised him. But where, I wondered. I had no money except my terminal pay and that was nearly gone. I didn't even talk very good English, but I knew Spanish and I liked kids. So I prayed hard, 'Oh God, this is an emergency. You gotta help me!' I told the Enchanters' leader, 'Meet me down by the River tomorrow morning at ten.'

"I didn't think he'd show but he did. Him'n other kids from the gang was lugging big shopping bags full of hardware. Did you know how to make a real gun out of a kid's toy?" Ramon asked me. "Look!" He reached into his desk drawer, drew out the kind of ten-cent-store pistol a small boy wears to play cowboy. "You tape it up this way. It shoots only one bullet but," Ramon added grimly, "one can be enough. We had to stop the neighborhood dances in our church basement after a boy was shot. The Enchanters felt kind of naked without their guns, now deep down in the River. How were they gonna protect themselves from the other gangs?

" 'Don't worry!' I told 'em. But me, I was worryin' plenty. 'La Viela wants out; she's too old to tend the candy shop. Maybe we can arrange to meet there.'

"Their faces brightened some. I rushed on. 'We need a new name. Any of you got any ideas?'

"*The Conservatives* was what the gang came up with. Now it was up to me to deliver their new clubhouse. The candy store was good because they were used to it; but where would I get the cash to pay the rent? I prayed harder than ever and inside of a week, a miracle happened. A swell dame from uptown collected the rent money from among her friends and we were in business. The Conservatives painted the wooden blinds bright silver and some of them put their hand prints on the wet paint to show they weren't chicken. The first thing you saw when you opened the door was the big sign MEMBERS ONLY.

"Each member paid only twenty-five cents a week, a dollar a month, if he had it," Ramon went on. "We fixed up some kind of jazz for every night in the week; walk in there about eight and kids were playin' their banjos and singin', some tossin' the basketball around, some playin' at an old pool table someone gave us. Maybe Monday night we had a pool tournament; Tuesday a discussion group about how we could help clean up some kid's street block; maybe Wednesday, they brought their girl friends for a sock dance with the record player. You name it, we did it. To belong to the Conservatives got to be a big thing—a what-do-you-call-it?"

"A status symbol?" I offered.

"Si, si." When Ramon is excited he lapses naturally into the Spanish he speaks with his Puerto Ricans, though he has Negroes, Italians, and Jews in his Conservatives, too. Ramon introduced a new kind of gang warfare. "When a guy from another gang'd call one of my kids 'chicken,' I'd say right back, 'You wanna fight? Meet us out back of the school house this afternoon at five. Only no guns or knives, just fists.' So they got it outa their systems while I refereed: I never told who won."

Keeping his mouth shut whatever happens is one of the chief reasons for Ramon's success with his gang, which now, ten years later, numbers 125 boys and girls who have a bigger clubhouse on Second Avenue. "They get along pretty good," Ramon said proudly. "The girls are the hardest to handle.

"Girls can hide the gang's guns in their skirts. They know the cops don't like to manhandle a girl," he explained. "It might get into the newspapers. Whatever they do, I never spilt even to a kid's mother or father, nor especially to any cop. Even the drug pushers know that I don't squeal on no one, so when I say, 'Listen, Johnny's mother is sick 'n they need food, not horse. Lay off him, will yah?' Sometimes he does. Even a pusher is human. Maybe he's got a family, too."

Youngsters know they'll get a straight answer from Ramon about anything that troubles them, however intimate. Recently he heard a young girl shrieking frantically in the club lavatory, "I'm bleedin' to death! Come, quick!" Ramon told her, "Congratulations! You just became a lady." When his boys get VD, he takes them to the hospital for a shot of penicillin. Facts are facts in East Harlem; you face them, go on from there, if you are the father of as big a family as Ramon has. Last year he wrote a letter to the mayor of New York City explaining, "Dear Mayor, we need some help." He got it and was able to hire a public school gymnasium after hours for his basketball team to practice in. "The Notre Dame team sent us their cast-off uniforms," Ramon beamed. "My boys won't even cut 'em down to size they're so proud of 'em." Ramon also gets jobs for his gang as a messenger on Wall Street, or maybe on Seventh Avenue in the wholesale dress district. One girl trained to become a registered nurse; one former Conservative just home from a hitch in the Navy made the most startling request, 'Ramon, can you help me get onto the Force?' Ramon explained, "To East Harlem kids, snakes and cops mean about the same. But they don't hate this one because he's their own."

The money from the city was rapidly running out when I talked with him, but Ramon's belief in miracles is still unshaken. He asked me, "You live in Boston? You know the

Kennedys?" I said doubtfully that, well, I'd gone to high school with the President's uncle but that hardly made me a friend of the family—but nowhere is too high for Ramon to go for help when it's for his kids. "They're nice people. They got a big family, too," Ramon insisted. "You tell 'em about my kids, hunh?" So now I am keeping my promise.

Even Sunday Schools in East Harlem Parish can be exciting, for each child has the sharpened wits of one who has had to fight the kid next door for his lollypop since they both wore diapers, who tomorrow may walk a Freedom March to force the public school authorities to hire a teacher who knows a little more than her pupils. One bright Sunday morning just before Easter I slid quietly into a seat in the basement of the Church of the Ascension where some sixty boys and girls under twelve were squirming from the unwonted starchiness of their best clothes. They were singing a Negro spiritual:

> Jesus walked this lonesome valley,
> He had to walk it by Himself,
> Oh, nobody else could walk it for Him,
> He had to walk it by Himself.
>
> We must go and stand our trial,
> You have to stand it by yourself,
> Oh, nobody else can stand it for you,
> You have to stand it by yourself.
>
> We must walk this lonesome valley,
> We don't walk it by ourselves,
> Somebody else has walked it for us,
> We don't walk it for ourselves. Amen.

It was announced that a class would put on a play which they had dramatized themselves. Immediately a fist fight broke out up in the front of the room with a bunch of boys hitting at each other, dodging, whacking wildly. This a Sunday School lesson? Finally they all filed off, beaming. Bewildered, I asked the small girl next to me whose hair was done up in about twenty neat pigtails tied with red ribbons, "What was that all about?"

She explained patiently, "The one who didn't hit anyone back was a Christian." She pointed up to a fish drawn on the blackboard in front of us. "That's Ichthus, fish. It stands for Jesus Christ the Son of God. *He didn't hit anyone. He was the one who got hit.*"

Greco-Christian philosophy from a nine-year-old in East Harlem! I've heard long sermons I'd gladly swap for what that child said. As I left they were singing again their Easter Anthem:

> The Son of God, He lived to save
> In a borrowed stable and a borrowed grave.

The most encouraging news about East Harlem, however, is the success of a large and determined group of people who live there to help themselves, who have discovered on their own initiative that they can actually have a say in the rebuilding of their own neighborhood. The Metro North Citizens' Committee started in the East Harlem Parish and Mrs. Millie Ryan, secretary of the very modern Church of the Resurrection, is also the efficient secretary of the Citizens' Committee. (Metro North is short for North of the Metropolitan Hospital on 96th Street.) Mrs. Ryan has lived on East 103rd Street since she was five years old and her roots there run deep.

Her dark eyes are passionately earnest as she points out, "Home is where your people are. I don't want to leave here, ever."

The first thing the Citizens' Committee did was to introduce Negro and Puerto Rican neighbors, shy of language differences, to each other, as they would work together. Then block chairmen were appointed to oversee local conditions, and finally even house chairmen took over, not only to try to make owners fix up the antiquated buildings but to plan how they themselves would improve health and cleanliness in their own neighborhood. Encouraged at the results, the Citizens' Committee went directly to the New York City Rent and Rehabilitation Committee to announce boldly, "We want to have a say about what will happen in our own block, not have buildings torn down and rebuilt with such big rents we can't afford them. We want to see the plans; find out how much apartments are going to cost when they're fixed up. These are our *homes*. Take old folks who got no money, no place to go, leaving tears their hearts out. Our block committees will help move them to some other rent temporarily, *but they gotta have the privilege of coming back home.*"

The rather dazed city authorities, only too glad to have the cooperation of the East Harlem residents themselves, agreed to cooperate financially while the federal government and a charitable foundation came into the picture with more necessary funds. The Citizens' Committee even had a hand in picking out their own architect for the building that will be completely renovated in the neighborhood of the Church of the Resurrection, the only East Harlem Parish brick building with all modern facilities, which is the pilot project of the proposed apartment reconstruction on surrounding blocks. City Hall reacted quickly, enthusiastically.

"The mayor himself came down here to our church to see our new plans. We were on TV!" Millie Ryan said proudly. "We're going to have bathrooms that work in the new apartments, bedrooms big enough so the kids won't have to sleep with the old folks, closets like we have never had before."

As George Metcalf wrote in *The Reporter:* * "This is probably the first time that a program initiated, planned and sponsored by a community has been accepted for a below-

* Quoted from "Metro North Moves Mountains," published by *The Reporter Magazine*, New York (November 17, 1966).

market, long-term, nonprofit rehabilitation of tenement buildings." Which is a carefully legal way of saying that the rents of the new tenements on seven blocks will be geared to the price the East Harlem people can pay who have an average yearly income of $3,700 and down. The experiment proves that tenement dwellers and city and federal government officials can actually trust each other and work together.

Most important of all to Millie Ryan and to thousands of other concerned mothers like her is the self-respect and pride that comes from knowing that even a comparatively small group of determined men and women can get things done in East Harlem. Unconsciously she straightened her broad, capable shoulders as she said, "We're going to have a place where my four kids can grow up, proud like other Americans."

"They need to give for their own sakes," Shanti Solomon had explained about her village women, half a world away in India. They too had experienced hunger, dirt, and despair, the humiliation of always receiving. They might never know it, but through the Fellowship of the Least Coin, prayers from all over the world were helping American children to sing in truth, "Land of the Pilgrims' pride."

Three

The Cross and the Lotus

THE LEAST COIN

With careless hand I gave the coin,
It seemed as nought to me.
The least of all my goodly share
As gift? A mockery!

My sister in her distant land
Gave one least coin, like me;
But went without her evening bread
To share her poverty.

Within the cup which feeds Thy lambs,
Our coins became, through Thee,
The golden coin of Fellowship—
Thy love—the alchemy.

SARA LINDSAY

THE MYSTERY of the East is being read with new glasses by the Christians of the West, with the Fellowship of the Least Coin helping workers from several nations to furnish the bright new lenses. Such a temple of mutual enlighten-

51

ment is the study center of Tao Fong Shan, which glitters and gleams from the very top of a lovely mountain outside Hong Kong. Here on a typically oriental architecture of bright red and gold with its pagoda roof are painted in golden Chinese characters the sayings of Jesus rather than those of Buddha. Here the cultures of ancient China and that of Europe and the United States can meet in peace under the Cross. What happens at Tao Fong Shan may well change the course of history.

For the reader to understand how exciting this Buddhist-Christian conversation is, it is necessary to explain how this most modern missionary adventure could flourish in this particular city dependent on China for most of its water and food and yet governed by the British. Hong Kong is one of the most beautiful, the most diverse, the most uneasy cities in the world. As your plane circles the lovely, intensely blue harbor, surrounded by sentinel peaks, you glimpse below the shipping of many nations; long lean destroyers from Europe, Asia, and America, giant passenger ships stuffed with bargain-hungry tourists, cargo vessels bristling with cranes as big as dinosaurs, swarms of white ferry boats fussing busily between Kowloon and Victoria Island, and, most numerous, the food junks from Red China loaded with vegetables and (underneath) agents and spies who thus slip verdantly past British patrols in a heap of lettuce. Like an arm stretched out into the sea lies the single long landing runway for the great jet upon which you ride; and you wonder how cold is the South China sea.

For a gray fog of fear hangs over this city, which is over ninety percent Chinese, where millions of penniless refugees and not a few millionaires, whether housed in mansions on the fashionable Peak or in miserable huts thrown together from packing boxes, live under the apprehension that this may be the day when Red China will take back Hong Kong. One American missionary explained, "Living in this beleaguered city is a daily gamble with death or at best with freedom versus slavery, for we older people who have been occupied by the Japanese military know all about prison camps. The only reason China has allowed Hong Kong to exist as a free city is that it is a gold mine; she needs for her own development its dollars, pounds, and francs."

I have visited many times this fascinating city where I have two adopted Chinese "daughters" whose school work and happiness I have supervised with love, but when we landed there in the spring of 1967 during the monsoon season, for the first time I was really afraid. A thick blanket of clouds muffled the harbor with its jagged peaks so that our plane circled, droning round and round, hoping for a break in the overcast. Finally the intercom barked, "We are going in. Please fasten your seat belts tightly, remove all glasses. This is merely a precaution. There is nothing to fear." But every passenger on that plane sensed this was "for real." No one spoke, coughed or moved from his crouch behind the seat in front of him, but as we roared down toward the single unseen runway, we could see through the window a threatening peak so near it seemed as if you could reach out and touch it. When the wheels of our plane touched down safely, the held breath from a hundred throats was released in a great gasp of relief.

As I moved shakily toward the ramp to disembark I told the hostess, "Please thank the captain for doing a wonderful job."

"And how!" she said fervently.

So does all Hong Kong live, a Christian worker (who would not even enter a Red Chinese store with me for fear of starting a riot) explained, with thankfulness that another day has been granted them. With American jets bombing only sixty seconds from the Vietnam-Chinese border, the precarious peace may easily erupt into a war of annihilation which might well wipe out both victor and vanquished, helpless civilians of both East and West. Even as I write, turmoil and violence has again exploded in the

crowded streets of Hong Kong; perhaps by the time this
account is published the Red guns under the lettuce will
have taken over. But this I do know; there live in that vast
city great Christian spirits who will never be conquered,
men and women who have lived so long with war and con-
quest that they take them in their stride as natural catas-
trophes like flood and typhoons, who will go on to the end
believing that all nations are truly brothers in the great
family of the same loving Father. Thus, modern Christianity, while giving up no jot or tittle of its belief, says to Buddhism and other Oriental religions not, "I am all right and
you are all wrong" but "Let us reason together. Perhaps out
of our mutual good we can build a new and peaceable
kingdom."

So many Eastern concepts are incomprehensible to the
Westerner staring horrified through the eyes of television
world newscasts, which see much that is overt, explain little
of the background culture to the viewer in his easy chair.
The American, munching TV snacks, wonders why does
that Buddhist monk douse himself with kerosene, burn himself up on the streets of Vietnam? What does he accomplish? If the Hindu is starving in India, why doesn't he grab
one of those skinny cows or monkeys which are eating up
his garden, have a good meal? If he is too stubborn to do this,
why should we bother to send him wheat? The "Yak, yak,
yak" of our Western "bop" music is equally incomprehensible to the Buddhist monk chanting age-old sutras (though
Eastern "now" adolescents love our noisy rhythms). The
average watcher of the silver screen in New Delhi is un-
aware that our Western movies are merely escape entertainment and that Jesse James has been long buried.

Yet scholars have unearthed many prayers and poems,
concepts of Eastern religions which might well have been
said from a modern Western Christian pulpit. Take, for
example, the inspired words of the Persian poet (1207-1273
A.D.), Jelel-ed-din Mevlana:

"You say the sea and its waves; but in so saying you do not mean two different things, for the sea, in its rising and falling, makes waves, and the waves, when they have fallen, return to the sea. So it is with men, who are the waves of God; they are absorbed after death unto him."

East and West meet harmoniously also in the red and gold temple on top of the mountain at Tao Fong Shan, the Hong Kong Christian Study Center on Chinese Religion and Culture, which the Least Coin Fellowship has helped to sponsor.

Translated from the Chinese, Tao Fong Shan means "The wind, the way and the mountain." Or Fong may be called more poetically "the wind of the spirit that bloweth where it listeth."

The feathery bamboos that lined the winding mountain road up which our small red car was panting one April morning, swayed to the invisible wind. Finally we halted with a squeak of relief in front of the gorgeous red and gold Buddhist temple. Its round painted columns, lovely curved pagoda roof, and gold-leafed doorway looked as if at any moment there might come down the shallow steps an orange-robed, barearmed priest of our Lord Buddha. Instead, a Christian Chinese priest in dark Western clothes came smiling to welcome us, to translate the gold Chinese characters over the doorway as THE HOLY TEMPLE OF CHRIST.

"Fifty ex-Buddhists come up from the valley to worship here every Sunday," the Christian priest explained. "They feel more at home amid their own background. We never have argued nor tried to proselytize; we simply try to explain that beauty is the common heritage of all religions, and that upon the best of the Chinese culture as well as that of the West may be erected the temple of Jesus Christ."

He went on quietly, "500 years before Christ, Gautama Buddha enunciated his own Golden Rule, that hatred does not cease by hatred at any time; hatred ceases by love—just as the philosopher Confucius explained that a gentleman would never 'do unto others what you do not wish to be

done to yourself.' Jesus's admonition to 'love your enemies
. . . pray for them that despitefully use you' went a step
further." Buddha did indeed kiss the leper and call him
"Brother," I recalled. But, to the Buddhist, loving his neighbor is a step in the giver's own progress toward perfection,
so that in his rebirth in the next life he may advance in the
scale perhaps from a mouse to an elephant, from a begger
to a *bodhisattva,* a "becoming Buddha." But the Christian
is adjured to love his neighbor *for his own sake,* even if
he is an enemy. Such love does not expect to be rewarded
but is, like that of the Good Samaritan, pure compassion.
Father Damien, who gave his life for those afflicted with the
dread disease of leprosy, belongs to this Good Samaritan
breed.

The priest of this gorgeous red and gold temple at Tao
Fong Shan waved a hospitable hand, invited, "Do come inside."

The columns that held up the painted roof were typically
Oriental as was the ornate altar, but above this hung a Cross
in three colors. "The black symbolizes sin," the priest explained. "Red is for the cleansing blood of the Lamb, and
white for purity, when sin is washed away." The gold which
flashed everywhere from the sun-lighted windows of this
Christian Oriental Temple, "reflects the Easter rejoicing
for victory over death." Outside, under the eaves, I saw hang-
ing a strangely engraved bell, "the largest ever cast in Hong
Kong," upon whose curving bronze rises a Christian Cross
growing out of the lotus blossom, the Buddhist symbol for
the beauty of the spirit. So, believe the scholars at Tao Fong
Shan, out of ancient philosophy may blossom the love of
Christ.

"Is it necessary for a Christian to make a complete break
with the past?" asks Bishop R. O. Hall, who came to Hong
Kong to head up this study of the three dominant religions
in Chinese culture, Buddhism, Taoism and the moral pre-
cepts of Confucianism. He was elected bishop of the Anglican

Church but he still lives stubbornly in his modest home on the top of Tao Fong Shan mountain, with all the valley spread out at his feet. He searches for the answer to the question, "Where can we see Christ's footsteps in the culture patterns of the past?"

This Christian Mission to the Buddhists was started by three Scandinavian countries, Denmark, Sweden and Norway, in 1956, the same year when Shanti Solomon first dreamed of the Fellowship of the Least Coin. When tribal and national customs crumble under the impact of modern political economic and scientific ideas, new standards must take the place of the old whether they be those of Mao Tsetung or those of Christ. A Basuto proverb puts it: "If a man does away with his traditional way of living and . . . his good customs, he had better first make certain that he has something of value to replace them."

The Fellowship of the Least Coin believe that researchers can discover at Tao Fong Shan "something of value." As Bishop Hall agreed in "Trying to Understand Our Own Times in Asia," * . . . our concern is not merely with the Christian Church "but with relation of the Creator to his creation, both in individual life and in the social patterns of the family, in the whole culture of a people, and among nations."

The family, he pointed out, "is a way in which God has spoken to and has taught ordinary people all through the centuries to live for someone else and not for themselves. How deeply and truly China has learned that lesson! How much she has to teach other nations of its vital importance . . . Families cannot survive without self-giving—nor can cities or nations."

China under Communism has tried to substitute for this ingrained family loyalty obedience to the state that can do no wrong. But may not the unexpectedly widespread unrest

* *Ching Feng* magazine, Volume IX, Number Two, Fall, 1966. Published in Hong Kong.

all over this vast country be an indication that underneath all this noisy upheaval, something of Old China still survives? Otherwise what would there be for these Red Guard children to fight? May not this great and ancient country, like the Prodigal Son, come to herself, return to the old disciplines, interpreted perhaps in a more modern Christian context, but still essentially Chinese? The Fellowship of the Least Coin hope that such a way may be found and are investing their prayers and tiny coins to help to this end.

Religion and commerce, culture and big business are not necessarily competitors but may be co-workers for better understanding. The laity in every nation have a responsibility, equal to that of the ordained priest, to live as Christians in business, the home and the community. "I suspect that Saint Paul would not have been able to go to Rome if it had not been for Rome's need of corn and other necessities in Asia Minor," Bishop Hall points out. "Similarly the first Christians in South China were probably Armenians and Syrians who came with Arab traders to Canton in the seventh century . . . When the Western world came to trade with the East in more modern times, the missionary movement followed. . . . Every time you pray 'Give us this day our daily bread' you take account of what God is doing through international trade."

It is not even necessary for a Buddhist to become Christian to recognize how valuable in mere dollars and cents is character based upon the Sermon on the Mount. When Bishop Hall was trying to raise money for support of the Chinese Christian bishops who, with their congregations scattered by Communism, with no support from overseas, were penniless, he was surprised when the non-Christian head of a great bank which has many branches in Hong Kong sent him a substantial contribution. The bank chairman explained, "We have our own private grading system for selecting new members for our staff: (a) Christians from Christian colleges; (b) non-Christians from Christian colleges; (c) Christians from government colleges; (d) non-Christians from government colleges."

"No one knows exactly what is happening to the native Christians inside China today," the Protestant priest at the Christian Temple for Buddhists at Tao Fong Shan admitted sadly. "But recently someone sent me this." He handed me a torn piece of a poster, smuggled out of inland China, headed with the words: *The Ten Sins of the Christians*. The priest added hopefully, "Some of them must survive or there would be no need of this."

In addition, the Least Coin Fellowship help provide bread and shelter in Hong Kong for "tuberculosis cripples," men too old or too twisted by disease to go out into the community to work but who in their rooms can do light handiwork, weaving or embroidering which is such a gracious art in this mecca for tourists sniffing for bargains. "Older people have such a hard time in these days when their families no longer feel responsibility for them," deplored one Hong Kong resident. "You can say that again," agreed an American. "It's the same at home, too."

But to me, staring down the lovely mountainside to the green and brown valley below where any day now new terror might break out, Tao Fong Shan was the most encouraging ecumenical adventure I knew about. With calm patience the Christian priests and scholars and as well as laywomen in the churches of Asia, Europe and America were looking beyond the fear and strife of today to a lasting peace based upon mutual understanding and tolerance. This small candle of faith in the power of Christ to fuse ancient and modern good into one Cross, may be a mere "burning in the dark," but it "gives a lovely light."

A practical woman of faith is a resident of Hong Kong, Rayann Ma (Mrs. John Ma). She took Shanti Solomon's place on the Fellowship Team in 1956; she has been a leader in the spread of the Fellowship of the Least Coin within the United Church of China.

Rayann learned about war along with her ABC's. Seeking desperately for a safe place to bring up their growing family as the Japanese menace grew, Rayann's parents took her as a small child from Swatow, where she was born, to Hong Kong, a free city. But safety and peace proved an illusion. When the banners of the Rising Sun were hoisted over Hong Kong on Christmas Eve, 1941, Rayann, a teenager, escaped from the city hidden in a junk; together with six businessmen, she walked for a week till she finally arrived, exhausted but triumphant at Canton, where the Union Theological Seminary had a spreading campus and buildings. She had barely registered for classes, however, before the Japanese juggernaut rolling at their heels forced both students and faculty to gather up what books and equipment they could carry and trek to Kukong. When this city, too, was threatened, the students once more shouldered their meager belongings and streamed across the barren hills, hiding from bandits as well as Japanese, arriving finally at a small village in the western province of Kwantung, where the courageous seminarians at once reopened classes.

"In those days a student had to fight literally not figuratively for his education," Rayann smiles reminiscently.

Conquerors might come and go but Latin and young love went on forever. John Ma was a senior at the seminary when Rayann arrived as a freshman but by the time he grasped his crackling new diploma, these two were engaged to be married in the modern manner as partners in building a new home. Mutual affection was the go-between rather than the family, when she went to marry him in Hong Kong.

"So I left behind my degree and became a triple Ma." Rayann smiles lovingly at her three children, a boy and two girls. Her John is today the pastor of a Hong Kong Congregational Church with three thousand members, where Rayann plays the organ for Sunday School, acts as hostess for the big parish, and teaches piano on the side to save cash for

her children's college education. Unlike the ordinary housewife and mother, however, she has served all over the world
as the voice for the inarticulate women of the mysterious
East. In 1958 she was elected the first chairman of the Asia
Christian Women's Conference, meeting in her home city.
She was one of the moving spirits who decided that the international small gifts of the Fellowship of the Least Coin
did not belong to any one country but must become the treasure of all women everywhere. As a delegate to the Assembly of the World Council of Churches, she traveled in
1961 to New Delhi, India; in 1966 she was chosen to go to
Kampala to help with the first All-Africa Women's Conference. During the same year, she flew to Tokyo to the
Third Asian Christian Women's Conference, where the
members of the Fellowship of the Least Coin were marveling
that after only ten years, their prayers now rose from around
the entire globe.

"Twenty-nine countries cover a lot of territory," Rayann
said soberly. "We must watch out that we remain humble.
We must not boast, saying 'Oh yes, look at us Asian women.
See what we do!' Now the Fellowship includes thousands
of other mothers, wives and sweethearts. It is not we who do
this great work of reconciliation but God through us. We
are but small channels burrowing through the debris of a
world in fragments. In our scientific era, who remembers
the power of prayer? Yet it can become an even greater
force if we are humble and sincere, truly believe that 'I can
do all things through Jesus Christ that strengtheneth me.'
Building prayer by prayer, small coin by small coin, we may
become true ambassadors for the Kingdom of Heaven on
earth, something we may have mumbled about every day
but may not really have believed in."

"I worry sometimes because my children have such a gad-
about mother, always going off to some other part of the
world," Rayann confesses. "But this has its good side too,

for it teaches them independence. When I leave, I tell my children, 'You will not always have me beside you. Any man or woman grows strong only by using his own muscles of body and mind.' " Small chance of these children taking to the drugs as prevalent in Hong Kong as in East Harlem! Rayann has given them self-respect and courage.

Rayann is the editor of the first Circle of Prayer, a collection of petitions written by women in Indonesia, Taiwan, India, the Philippines, the United States, Pakistan, Japan, Thailand, Korea and New Zealand for use by the Fellowship of the Least Coin in many countries. She also designed the circle of praying hands, the fingers of women touching to make an endless chain around the world, which has become the official seal of the Fellowship. In the center is the lotus flower which denotes spiritual beauty in the East. Thus, as each woman puts her monthly smallest coin into her bamboo stick, bright woven bag, or clay pot stuck on a mud wall, she may repeat the words of a woman thousands of miles away who is praying, too:

O God, thou art the father of all. . . . We thank thee that in Jesus Christ thou hast revealed thyself, and that through him, thou hast bestowed thy love on all mankind. . . . The hope of all the peoples of this earth is in thee.

O Master, soon after thy birth, thou didst become a refugee, a wanderer upon the road. To thee we would bring the tens of thousands of refugees who in our day are living in suffering. Wilt thou strengthen the sympathy in human hands, that man may be concerned to help man and that together all may share in thy mercy and love.

O God, because thou art the great Father of all, man does not need to be divided by race and nation for all are thy children. . . . All the world may become one big family. May the prayers of thy faithful children encircle our whole earth and may these prayers arise unceasingly day and night.

MRS. CHING MING LEE, *Hong Kong*

Another woman in Hong Kong who has a doctorate in English literature voiced the wistful yearning of Christians around the world to claim Jesus Christ as one of their own race, in spirit if not in body. "And why not?" she asked. "To the early Jews, Jesus was a fellow Jew; he became also one with the Gentiles. To the African he may be black or he may show a pale face to the Westerner. It makes small difference if the artist paints him as anaemic with a long flowing beard like the 'hippies' of today. The important thing is not the color of his skin or his haircut, but that the conversation with him . . . call it prayer if you like . . . becomes real communication. Then women in saris and in miniskirts speak the same language of reconciliation."

Rita Luk, secretary for women's work of the Church of Christ in China, is another Asian responsible for this "long look." She knows through experience that if your dream is big enough, it can come true, for she has watched it happen at Shum Oi (Deep Love), her heaven-soaring new home church.

Rita came to Hong Kong from mainland China as a high schooler and later became one of the few women elders of Shum Oi congregation. When the Japanese took over Hong Kong, the members had to scatter, but when peace came, they gathered again, crowded into a small storefront. They were invited to join a large missionary complex by building a new church which would cost $600,000, a fantastic sum for them to aspire to when many earned only fifty cents a day, Hong Kong, or ten cents, American. The 250 members decided that if they worked as hard as they could with faith, the money would come; but scrape and save as they might, they were still despairingly far from the required total when the wealthy owner of a textile mill quietly offered to double whatever sum they raised. With this assurance, the building was started, began to take shape. On Christmas Eve 1966, the congregation toiled till midnight to clear away the litter of lumber, shavings and dusty cement, to put into the shell of the new church the pews from the old. On Christmas morning the church was thronged with a triumphant congregation weeping and smiling, singing, "Joy to the world, the Lord is come!" The textile plant owner came beaming to Rita to ask, "Well, have I done all I promised?"

"Yes and more," Rita told him gratefully.

He went home from the thanksgiving service that Christmas morning and two hours later was dead. Rita, telling me this story, said quietly, "His family did not mourn. They said, 'He did what he wanted and then went to sleep.' Not every one has the satisfaction of seeing his dream come true in soaring stone. I wonder what he thinks when he looks down from heaven on a Sunday morning and sees us all gathered there, singing?" Like the other Christian women of Hong Kong, Rita is not afraid of anything that can happen to her in her home city. She says calmly, "I know that any day Red China takes over I may become a Christian martyr. But so have many others before me."

Rita designed the Hong Kong Fellowship's red, blue, and gold silken flag which is carried down the church aisle once a year, together with the church flag, when the Least Coins of the women of the Church of Christ in China are dedicated. The altar is piled high with small cardboard boxes heavy with tiny coins (worth one American penny). But the amount collected is not important, for in the dedication prayer, East and West, North and South become one. On the Hong Kong cardboard box is depicted the miracle of the loaves and fishes—the same Ichthus, the ancient Christian symbol beloved for two thousand years.

One Sunday evening I climbed five flights of dark concrete stairs to attend a service which the adolescents who live in these anthills they call home (a resettlement apartment teeming with twenty-five hundred Chinese) hold weekly in their rooftop chapel. When fire made shelterless fifty-four thousand refugees from China living in hillside shacks, city huts and the doorways of Hong Kong merchants, the British authorities put up these huge "resettlement" projects. The thousands of inmates do not live in luxury. Each family occupies one room, ten by twelve feet, in which must live five "units." A child under twelve counts for only half a unit, so to make up the required number, in this single room may live a father, mother, four small children plus a "boarder." In the public rooms, two water faucets are available for four hundred families. Yet the Chinese are such clean people that even the coolies who live huddled there wash every night not only themselves but their one suit of underwear, which is hung up on the iron railing to dry for morning. Since both parents usually have to work to buy rice for the family, they may lock up their room to keep out the thieves and leave only the streets for the children to play in. Or grandma may tend the baby too small to walk; it is a sight to watch on the narrow verandas that run in front of each door, a dozen Chinese babies splashing happily in as many basins.

"But what will the young people be like who come from these overcrowded homes?" I wondered as, guided by another American, I felt my way up the dark unlighted concrete stairs toward the roof. The meeting was late because the young people, ranging from fourteen to seventeen years of age, worked seven days a week in factories, plumbing businesses, garment-making lofts where, as apprentices, they made only a very small salary while they learned, but were fed their meals. As one of them explained gravely, "It is good to eat." The rooftop was surrounded with chin-high, heavy wire hopefully to discourage thieves, but you could look down through the meshes at the brightly lighted cement cubicles where life was as public as on the streets below. I watched a man bathing naked at the kitchen sink, a mother setting a steaming pot of rice upon a table where sat six children, a tailor sewing frantically upon his machine the dress that must be finished before the tourist ship left port tomorrow, a small student digging his fingers into his ears to shut out the tumult of sounds as he tried to master tomorrow's lesson, and a man and a woman in a top bunk with their arms around each other. Times Square in New York at dusk had nothing on this fierce clutching at life. Could Christianity have anything real to give to the children from such homes? Could all the Least Coins of the Fellowship piled mountain-high reach such a rooftop?

The leader of the service that evening was seventeen. He had worked all day in a textile mill before he changed into his neat dark-blue suit and his immaculate white shirt; yet he looked very much like a student ready for dinner at the American private school which my own son had attended. His ingrained Chinese courtesy welcomed us two Americans as he led us to a seat, though he spoke no English. The hymn book he handed us was very old, printed in Shanghai at a time when Christians were still tolerated. The choir, boys and girls in white surplices over their much-washed cotton dresses and black trousers, came in singing the hymn of my own childhood:

> Jesus, Lover of my soul,
> Let me to Thy bosom fly,
> While the nearer waters roll
> And the tempest still is high . . .

As they sang in Chinese, I sang the remembered words in English with a nostalgic lump in my throat. The tempest might soon become high indeed, the uneasy streets below us erupt into Communist violence. But these Christian boys and girls were not afraid. They had what the world needed most, something to believe in, to hope for, a goal worth living and if necessary dying for.

> Other refuge have I none,
> Hangs my helpless soul on Thee.
> Leave, ah, leave me not alone . . .

They were not alone. For the wind of the spirit blew as strongly up here on this rooftop as on the high mountain at Tao Fong Shan. And the hard-earned coins in their collection plate were not only for themselves but to help others.

Shanti Solomon had once commented quietly, "An inch of giving adds a foot of self-respect."

Even a child in East Harlem or in Hong Kong can understand such simple arithmetic. As I left the tiny chapel on top of the government apartment house in whose lighted cubicles swarmed so many hundreds of men, women, and children, I had to go out through the adjoining rooftop school room where the teacher was preparing tomorrow's lessons. Curious, I picked up from her desk a small cardboard box which had printed on its side the same Ichthus, the fish which the little girl with the red-ribboned pigtails in East Harlem had told me stood for Jesus Christ, the Son of God. Only one small coin rattled, lonely inside the box.

The teacher explained, "Yesterday thieves cut through the wire on our roof here and stole my Least Coin box which was almost full, from my desk. Most of our children are lucky if they get two meals a day but I keep my box there because they love to drop in a coin for 'children who do not have as much as we do.' What thief would be so low-down as to steal the Least Coin box? Consternation and indignation ran high. To calm them down, I found another box for my desk but it was, of course, empty. This morning an excited beaming seven-year-old boy rushed up to me, shouting, 'Do not worry! My mother, when she went to work, left me this ten cents so I could eat rice.' He dropped the coin into the slit in the new box. 'See, Least Coin, I have given you my breakfast!' "

Four

Harambee – Let Us Work Together

NAIROBI, where the Fellowship of the Least Coin is also investing its prayers and "widow's mite," is doubly thrilling for a New Englander to visit, for not only is it a clean and beautiful city of tall white buildings and wide boulevards gorgeous with tropical flowers, but it is 1776 all over again; the exciting, vibrant democracy is so new you can still smell the varnish. As our farmer ancestors rushed to Concord and Lexington to "fire the shot heard round the world," as we painted upon our improvised flag the snake with the warning, "Don't tread on me!", just as passionately three hundred thousand Kenyans roared, "Uruhu! Freedom!" when in 1963 the Union Jack slid down the flagpole at the great stadium at Nairobi and the bright new Kenyan flag rose proudly to the vast blue sky.

"The new National flag is composed of three broad stripes, black, red and green, separated by narrow white stripes, with crossed spears and a shield superimposed in the center. The top black stripe represents the people of Kenya; red represents the struggle for freedom; and the green, Kenya agriculture and natural resources. The white stands for unity and peace, while the shield symbolizes the defense of freedom."

The second rousing Kenyan shout is "Harambee! Let us

69

work together!" The great hunger for education has resulted in dirt-floored little rough wooden schoolhouses very like those in which our Puritan boys and girls squeaked their pencils across their slates. Since the brand-new government was too poor to provide enough schools immediately, the anxious parents not only erected the Harambee schools with their own hands but out of their meager income paid trained teachers so that their young could learn more about what was happening in the great world of nations of which they had now become new proud peers.

The Christian Church is also pioneering in Kenya. On Easter morning as I attended service at one of the first such churches in the Masai Reserve, the red-robed, tall, bare-legged men of the congregation stacked their murderously sharp spears outside the church door very much as my own ancestors had stacked their muskets which they had carried against the Indians, when they went inside to pray.

The spirit of 1776 and 1963 had much in common; both New Englanders and Kenyans hated the English for their stubborn belief that they "were the people destined to rule the earth" and at the same time secretly admired their dogged industry and knowledge that brought fertility to the bare brown hills. The British can be exasperating rulers but steadfast friends. The important difference between the rebel New Englanders and the Kenyan patriots was that instead of being of the same blood and background as the British newcomers, the Africans stemmed from a vastly different culture. Approximately fifty different tribes, each with its own language and customs, make up the new East African Republic and the vital problem of Jomo Kenyatta, the George Washington of his country, is how to unite into one great nation these varied peoples.

The bitterness between blacks and whites because of the atrocities perpetrated by hoodlums who took over the Mau Mau fight for freedom is not easily forgotten, nor are the nine years of Kenyatta's imprisonment. Historians record that fewer than one hundred English plantation owners and their families were butchered during what they called, with typically British understatement, "The Emergency," during which women had to tote revolvers along with their lipsticks to save their lives and those of their children. Few realize that over thirteen thousand black Kenyans, Christians and non-Christians, were also "pangaed to death," killed because they refused to take the Mau Mau oath. Mrs. John Gatu, whose husband is now the efficient and beloved General Secretary of the Presbyterian Church of East Africa, spent a night of horror up a tree, with her hand fearfully held over the mouth of her youngest child lest he make a sound which would betray them to the Mau Mau fanatics raging below, for discovery meant certain death.

The experience of Priscilla Mereka and her family, who lived in a farmhouse outside Thika (famous for its flame trees) is typical of what can happen when ugly passions run riot. Priscilla, a worker among Christian women in far-flung village churches, and her husband, John, who taught in a mission school, both knew that their refusal to take the Mau Mau oath might eventually be their death knell. One night that thing which they feared came upon them when the very neighbors with whom their children played daily arrived armed with spears and pangas (great curved knives which the natives use for nearly everything, as hoes, weapons, or as gadgets to clean their fingernails). The community not only beat up brutally the whole Mereka family, but killed Priscilla's visiting brother-in-law when he protested. "Friends of years' standing stole everything we had, clothes, furniture, food; they cleaned us out. We limped and crawled to the mission compound, glad to have escaped with our lives . . . except for my poor brother-in-law," Priscilla relates, quietly matter-of-fact. After "The Emergency" was over, both Merekas began to teach again at the re-opened mission school. "These same parents who had attacked us sent their children back to our classes but I noticed that they avoided me, as if they were ashamed. So one evening at a PTA meeting I got up and said frankly, 'Christ has taught us to forgive. He has forgiven me. So I have forgiven you for what you did to me and mine. Please do not hesitate to come to me to ask how your children are doing in their studies. I will listen and answer.' "

Christians, who now compose about 20 percent of the five million Kenyans, are one of the great unifying forces in this new republic. Realizing that their teaching of the importance of the individual was one cause of the rising spirit of Kenyan independence, the courageous church people went fearlessly into the "detention camps," where anyone suspected of Mau Mau tendencies was confined behind barbed wire and thorn bushes; these brave Christians taught the saving peace of forgiveness. The resulting converts are the backbone of the indigenous Kenyan Christian churches today, for they understand that Christian principles cannot be imposed from without, but must grow naturally out of the roots of what is good in the culture of Kenya itself. They live their religion of tolerance and hope as the Merekas do.

Priscilla and her husband bought a new stone farm building and set up housekeeping in the old neighborhood but with new and bigger goals. Since Mr. Mereka is an agricultural expert, they planted their twenty-four acres with 5,000 coffee bushes; they increased the yield of their maize fields from ten to twenty-five bags an acre by the use of modern fertilizer. Intent upon creating a fund which would send her four sons to college, Priscilla insisted upon planting a hundred macadamia trees, which take six years to bear fruit but whose luscious much-sought-after nuts will bring in a tidy sum eventually. Since meat is expensive, she and her husband have dug a fish pond at the foot of the hill upon which their farmhouse stands, to supplement their diet with plenty of protein. Their next-door neighbor is now digging a similar pond fed from a nearby brook and has asked the Merekas to order him a load of fertilizer like theirs.

"What we need in every village is another Priscilla!" commented the agricultural government expert from Nairobi.

Priscilla's household like that of all Kikuyus welcomes every member of her family, however remote, and is as gay as Christians are supposed to be. Priscilla's small niece, Susan, whom she adopted when her sister died in childbirth, sings as naturally as a bird. A small happy child of five in a short red dress, Susan stood up at the Mereka luncheon table and sang to us Americans:

> Jesus, friend of little children,
> Be a friend to me.
> Take my heart and ever keep me
> Close to thee.

When as we left, Priscilla laid her warm dark cheek against mine, drew in her breath in the Kikuyu greeting for a friend, I felt, as Shanti had in Manila, "a warmth about my heart." Like the sixty-five women, perfect strangers who had prayed for my safety on my "grand safari" to Vietnam, Africa has a great heart of love for those who come to her with understanding.

The Christian tolerance with which Priscilla treats the neighbors who killed her brother-in-law is reflected in many of the compassionate English who still remain in Kenya as citizens.

"This is my country, too. I was born here and I intend to stay," insisted one English woman whose family has lived in Nairobi for three generations. "My husband and I are even building a new house! Some people think this insane, but whatever of know-how we have is needed now as never before to develop our new nation. There are difficulties, yes, with ignorant people who are still 'feeling their oats'; but Jomo Kenyatta with remarkable tolerance has made it clear that we who love Kenya are still welcome here as citizens, whatever the color of our skins. Perhaps if we live our religion, we can make this the first truly Christian democracy.

Certainly Europe and America with their wars and bombs have not yet earned that title."

Thousands of Kenyans hold this same hope for the future though they may not use the word "Christian." The Speaker of Parliament is an Englishman whom everyone trusts since, as one black Kenyan puts it, "When our factions get to quarreling, we know he will always be strictly fair." The Scottish secretary of agriculture has tried several times to resign but his fellow Kenyans won't let him; they argue that his wisdom is needed desperately to bring back to fruition the coffee plantations left by departing Englishmen, to teach modern agricultural methods and to build up financial security for the new state.

Kenyatta himself is not a member of the Christian Church. He is a lusty man who has already enjoyed four wives but he has legally divorced each spouse before marrying the next one, which according to Kikuyu tribal custom he did not have to do. While distrusting the actions of many Christians who do not live up to their beliefs, he does not forget that Presbyterian missionary doctors saved his life when at the age of ten he was stricken with a serious spinal disease. The exact date of his birth is uncertain but he recalls proudly that in 1913 he was circumcised along with the rest of his adolescent tribal group, thus becoming officially a Kikuyu adult. His father's name was Kamau and the missionaries gave him the baptismal name of Johnstone; he himself took the name of Jomo (Burning Spear) Kenyatta and it is said that the colors of the new Kenyan flag are taken from the belt of black, red, white, and green which he wore when he roared on his motorcycle from Nairobi to the Kikuyu Reserve. (What a familiar sound that word has for the American Red Indian!)

To realize the task of modern Christian missions in East Africa it is necessary to understand political and social conditions in that very new democracy. President Kenyatta exemplifies both the fierce love of the land of his people and the tolerance that seeks to include all tribes and races in tomorrow's national growth. Strangely, many of the English who imprisoned him and called him "a Mau Mau murderer" are now his friends and co-workers.

As an angry young man, Kenyatta coveted the classical education of the Englishman. Accordingly, in 1929 he went to London to study at the university. But further Western education made him even more intensely a Kikuyu, fiercely loyal to his tribe. While in England he wrote *Facing Mount Kenya,** an explanation of Kikuyu culture not yet surpassed. Mt. Kenya, the holy "mountain of brightness" seventeen thousand feet high, cloud-crested and magnificent, is considered the home of the tribal god, Ngai. Kenyatta voiced eloquently the passionate love of his people for the good red earth, the "mother of us all." By tilling the fields the Kikuyu farmer lives, here he buries his sacred dead, and the earth is the only inheritance of his sons, both born and unborn. Kenyatta explained, "To swear by the earth is a mighty oath, for it nurses the spirits of the dead through eternity." We who purchased Manhattan from the Indians for $24 should understand his indignation when the English bought "for a pittance" the vast open fields which the black Kenyans were not cultivating but which the white man, planting coffee and sisal, soon turned into gold. To Kenyatta, these unused fields were merely rented by the English; they were no more "unowned land" than the open moors he had seen in England. He had no prejudice against the British as a race; he even married an English woman, but he divorced her in 1946 to return to the red earth of his native hills, more determined than ever that Kenya must be taken back by his people. Yet from his early Christian contacts may he not have gathered the germ of this tolerance which, as president of the new republic, he was to show to all races by allowing them to take equal citizenship in the new nation?

On the blackboard of the English class at the Harambee

---

* *Facing Mount Kenya* by Jomo Kenyatta, Mercury Books, London, 1936.

school to which Priscilla Mareka took me one morning was written the sentence to be parsed for that day, "No man shall be looked down upon because of his color or creed." The teacher could not possibly have known I was coming, although Priscilla was an old friend, for she comes weekly with other Christian women to clean and sew for the orphan children who live there. The Kenyan women feel strongly it is their job as well as the man's to help build the new nation. To test the youngsters' knowledge of English I offered to answer any questions. One boy's hand shot up.

"What country does your President Johnson come from?" he demanded.

I hesitated, then smiled. "From the great country of Texas, so big it takes about two hours in a jet plane to fly over," I told the boy. "Only we call it 'a state.' "

"The number of secondary schools in Kenya has been increased by 40 percent by these Harambee schools," the English teacher told me proudly. In addition to their book studies, these young people learn to make beautifully turned-out shoes (though few of the country pupils wear any, the shoes bring a good price in Nairobi) and the girls knit clothes, since a trade plus book knowledge makes jobs doubly sure when they graduate. The older children also act as tutors at home for the other six or seven children in their families, since the parents, who earn in a good season only fifteen hundred or two thousand shillings a year if the coffee crop is good, cannot afford to pay more than the six hundred shillings tuition charged for one child.

There were twenty orphans, seventeen of them boys, living in the dormitory of this school which Priscilla and I visited, where their balanced if barely adequate diet is supplied by the government. Many thousand more children were lost during the confusion and terror of The Emergency. These twenty knew why they were here in the school. With their arms stiffly held at their sides like good soldiers, they sang the national anthem (whose music used to be an old Kikuyu

lullaby) with loud, passionate voices and then these mother-
less and fatherless youngsters swung into plaintive melody,

> I wanna see my father 'fore I die . . .
> I wanna see my mother 'fore I die . . .

Of course they never will. But the state and good women
like Priscilla are their family as are the Indian pastor and
his wife who run the Eastleigh Community Center in one of
the worst crime-ridden, thickly populated sections of the
city of Nairobi. Like the Fellowship of the Least Coin which
helps Eastleigh this is an international cooperative venture,
English, Asians, and Americans helping Africans to help
themselves. Even the residents of Nairobi were upset when
they first learned where the Community Center was to be
started. Sent by the Church of North India, the first missionary pastor and his wife who moved there had been
warned by their neighbors in Poona that "The Mau Maus
will cut you up and eat you!" Unafraid, the Asian missionaries were met by the Nairobians who further protested,
"You don't want to settle there on the street of prostitutes!
Thieves flock there; men even murder for a few pennies.
We would not dare to send our children to your school in
this neighborhood nor to come ourselves."

"Jesus was a dangerous radical and the friend of Mary
Magdalene," the Indian Christian pastor said in his gentle
voice that masked an iron determination. "Where we are
most needed is where we must be." So the missionary family
set up housekeeping as planned with an open door for anyone in trouble.

There were (and still are) many houses of prostitution on
the street upon which stands the Eastleigh Christian Center,
whose church auditorium doubles on weekdays as a primary
school. Nursery school classes, made up in large part by the
children of these unmarried women, are housed in the Felicia
Sunderlal Memorial, built in her memory by gifts from all

over the world. The Fellowship of the Least Coin which she
fostered helps support the nursery school there for some
forty youngsters who arrive each morning, hungry. Many
of the prostitutes who send their children in order to get
them fed and off the streets are pregnant and proud of their
big bellies, since according to Kikuyu ancient belief, whoever the father, a woman is not fulfilled until she has a
child to add to the tribe. Urged to give up one of her
children for adoption by a family who could well afford to
give the boy every advantage, one such unmarried mother
objected fiercely, "But my children are my only riches!"
Married women are accustomed to being the chattel of the
male to whom, after the bride price is paid, she belongs as
much as his hut or his panga. "Mother" is considered the
most honorable tribal name and to be barren is a disgrace.
With such ingrained obedience to male authority, the woman
has to be taught that as an unwed female her body is her
own, that she can say, "No," if she wants to to any impor-
tunate male. Her children learn at Eastleigh that their
bodies are the temple of God to be kept untouched until
marriage.

When Felicia first visited East Africa, she was startled at the
tension generated between her people (Asians, as they are
called) and the native black Kenyans. Thousands of Indians
had lived in Kenya, generation after generation; in Nairobi
they were confined to a rather pleasant but prescribed area
not far from Eastleigh. Some were originally laborers who
had come to help build the railroad to Uganda, but who
later became by their industry such successful shopkeepers or
entered civil service in such numbers that they were re-
sented by the unskilled tribesmen who could find no jobs.
This gentle Indian girl with her compassionate brown eyes,
her gracious sari, became the symbol of international Christian concern for Indians and black tribesmen alike; to her
they were both wistful children, seeking their Father, God.
When I had met Felicia in New York City in 1961, she

had explained that the Fellowship of the Least Coin meant "Sisterhood of Prayer, conversation with God in many languages." When Felicia discovered she had incurable cancer, she did not panic, but merely extended this international Christian family to include eternity. She confessed to a group of women on Easter Day (1961) only five months before she died:

The eternal life has been a very real thing to me. The fear and unwillingness to enter it have evaporated. There is a sense of spiritual and beautiful excitement as to what that new life is to be; hence this life becomes more meaningful because it is a preparation for the next life. And whether we work here or there, we are working for Him all the time.

The Eastleigh Christian Center, which includes the memorial to this woman whose quiet faith shouted louder than trumpets, prides itself on being the first nonsegregated social service community project in Nairobi. As such, it has had the backing of the Kenya government. In this large square building, forty nursery school children each morning and forty others each afternoon work and sing under a wall painting sent by Felicia's friends in Czechoslovakia. At noon the commercial high school students clatter their typewriters there, and other young people studying trades or chemistry of the soil fling themselves into the comfortable armchairs to prepare their lessons for tomorrow. Nights, the young people present native dramas such as the folk tale of "The Lost Child," which they have dramatized themselves; their biggest hit has been acting out the marriage customs of the varied tribes of Kenya, which also meant original research of value for future historians. These youngsters play a "mean" guitar and drums for dancing. Felicia's big bright room belongs to all who have need of shelter, recreation, or peace. From the wall looks down a lovely Madonna painted in bright reds and blues by one of the African young people;

books line the other walls of this refuge for all the hungry the frightened, and the young people eager to learn. Each adolescent who is thus helped in his studies is himself required to teach someone younger than he, and so the endless chain of friendship and education goes on and on. The Memorial Building has been used for all kinds of emergencies. Here fifty refugees from the Sudan bedded down on their blankets for weeks until the Kenyan government could find for them more adequate accommodations. Loving kindness is the only key to the door of Felicia's House.

Frequently the pregnant girl who comes for help to the Eastleigh Center is only fifteen or even younger; she is never turned away. One woman whose husband had no job and who was driven to selling her body by her baby's crying for food was given rent and food money and trained in household management; a job was also found for her husband. The family is now back together and the baby was baptized by Rev. R. H. Ghatage, the Indian pastor of the two hundred-member congregation, who pushes back the curtain which hides the altar on weekdays and preaches every Sunday in Kikuyu, Swahili, and English. He regards the problems of the whole community as his, regardless of their creeds, and even finds time for trips across the borders of Tanzania and Uganda. "Three countries make quite an extended parish," I remarked, awed, but he merely smiled and quoted, "The world is my parish."

Sometimes the beneficiaries of Eastleigh are known only to God. Beside the Sunderlal Memorial stands a tall unpainted Cross, held erect by a tumbled pile of stones, which commemorates three unnamed Christian men, African, Asian, and American friends, who went into the angry tumult of the Congo rebellion to try to help and never were heard from again. The day I visited Eastleigh, seated on one of the largest unmarked stones was a small boy with a tin pail in his hand, waiting patiently for the milk that would be poured into it an hour later to assuage his thirst and hunger. He knew the milk would come; was he not in the shadow of the Cross? To me, he was the very symbol of modern Africa.

Mary Kirobi, who interpreted for me at the meeting at which sixty-five Kikuyu women asked to join the Fellowship of the Least Coin, and Mary Jane Patterson, an American Negro, are helping to carry on the work for former prostitutes. They have organized a school where teenage girls, not only from Nairobi but from surrounding towns, can learn skills other than the oldest profession—English necessary for employment, child care, sewing and such practical trades as box-making for a local factory. "If we can assure them of a job, we've got it made," explains Mary Jane. The Nairobi City Council, mindful of what Eastleigh has already done interracially, has donated the land, and it is hoped that by 1968 a brick building will rise beside the Sunderlal Memorial, large enough to accommodate forty such ambitious girls and their teachers.

"Our present biggest job is to convince the woman from the bush that she has a right to keep her body to herself," Mary Jane explains. "That she need no longer become the possession of the men of her tribe or any other. When I first came here to Nairobi, I was told, 'Your example is worth more than your words. Just go on being a black woman who is free to live a decent life of her own, to be the equal of any man.'"

In 1963 during the very early days of the new democracy, the Fellowship of the Least Coin further invested in the welfare of Kenyan children by paying the way of Miss Nebuko Minami, the head of the Hokuriku Kindergarten Teacher Training School, one of the most famous in Japan, to come to East Africa to train native nursery school teachers in the methods for which Japan is famous throughout the world. (Strangely, the Japanese in Kenya are classed as "Europeans"; only the Indians and Pakistani are labeled "Asians.")

An American kindergarten teacher, Mrs. Louise Leber, was associated with Miss Minami in setting up training courses for Kenyan students in both rural and city districts. They discovered great enthusiasm among the African students although conditions in which to work often proved primitive. The Matuga Training Center, to which fifty girls came to study, proved to be an old agricultural post where cow barns, sheds, and milking rooms had been converted into classrooms and dormitories. When all the beds were filled, the new girls stuffed gunny sacks with grass and said they "slept fine. What we are learning about teaching with imagination with the materials at hand is well worth any minor adjustments," they insisted. Miss Minami stayed in the home of a Quaker missionary who gave back the room and board money offered by her Japanese guest to buy pens, paints and certificates for the Kenyan children, since, the hostess explained, "I was not brought up to receive pay from guests in our home."

However, the Matuga nursery school was most grateful for boxes of toys sent for the children. "The wagon with bells inside its wheels, the foam rubber elephant, the little wooden railway cars and tracks, the dollies and baby bed, balls, and tortoise—they are loved and loved and you'll never guess how much unless you come over and see," reported the thank-you note to America.

"We had our nursery children's Sports Day where there were about two thousand people, children and spectators. The teams of children in bright sunsuits came in, competing for a cup. Some were dressed in red, some in yellow, some in blue, some in navy, some in green. They were so clean and beautiful and shiny. They played and danced and circles were formed in exercises done, until the crowd roared with approval."

The Ofafa Nursery School in Nairobi, in quarters donated by the YWCA with the teacher's salary paid by the Fellowship of the Least Coin, proved equally successful. Miss Minami wrote back to her own Hokuriku Gakuin (School) so enthusiastically about her two African nineteen-year-old assistants, Lornah Chayuga, daughter of the pastor in charge of the Friends' African Mission and Grace Munyiba, that the Japanese college faculty and the students decided to celebrate their eightieth anniversary by sponsoring further study in Japan for the two Kenyan girls. "Japanese kindergarten children as well as community organizations contributed to the funds raised by the Hokuriku girls to cover their travel from Nairobi. Scholarships were provided by the college for their tuition and living expenses. They took great pride in having 'the first Africans to study kindergarten training in Japan.'"

These gifts snowballed into larger service to small Kenyans even after Miss Minami went home. The two girls who, as junior college students, studied nursery and kindergarten education, psychology, piano, handicrafts, current events, and English literature as well as the Japanese tea ceremony and flower arrangement, came home to Nairobi very well-equipped. Grace, who is now married and has a young son of her own, Daniel, supervises a nursery school of eighty children under the Nairobi City Council.

When I visited the Ofafa Kindergarten School at the YW, now headed by Lornah Chayuga, a slight, gay girl who bubbled with as much vivacity as her small charges, forty youngsters held out their small hands, demonstrated that they had also used paste and toothbrushes and so were shining clean. They stay here at school all day while their parents are at work. Lornah teaches them Japanese games as well as their own tribal dances, and they can sing nursery songs in three languages.

She suggested to the children, "Perhaps you'd like to sing for our guest the story of the bee? First in Kikuyu, please, then in Japanese, then in English." The children sang heartily, and the final chorus of "Zum, Zum, Zum," needed no interpretation; obviously these youngsters were being taught that children in other countries were their friends.

As these small, gaily clad boys and girls tiptoed into the next room, carrying their own light cots for their morning nap, Lornah smiled when I asked who had painted the Easter story of the Resurrection upon the walls of the schoolroom. Were these children all Christians?

"Oh no. Some are; most are Moslems or Kikuyus to whom the altar for their ancestors is an important part of their home worship. I painted those . . . I hope you can tell Mary Magdalene from John, the Beloved! The children learn the alphabet, to count to one hundred, hygiene, English, but no dogma. We try to train them how to get along together whatever background they may have, because cooperation of all citizens is especially important in a country such as ours where many tribes must become a unit, politically and socially, if democracy is to work.

"If a child is quarrelsome we put him alone in the coat closet to think it over," Lornah explained. "He is told this is not just a punishment but a chance for him to think over how horrible it is to be disliked by other children. When he is ready to say 'Sorry' he can come out again to shake hands with the boy he has hit over the head with his toy engine. In a democracy even a child has to understand that his neighbor whom he dislikes (perhaps with reason) has rights as well as he." None of the children have any idea that the foster "mothers" in the Fellowship of the Least Coin who watch over him come from nations around the world. "Which," Shanti says calmly, "is as it should be. For those of us who have no sons like me, these boys and girls are our families."

In this way, even preschool Kenyan children are being trained in tolerance and in pride in their own culture and nation. This cultural integrity is also expressing itself in action in the present-day Christian church in East Africa;

acceptance of responsibility by laity and clergy alike has led to changes in procedure, both superficial and deep. The General Assembly of the Presbyterian Church of East Africa, headed by its modern, outstandingly tolerant Secretary, John Gatu, was in session when I was in Nairobi. Many of the wives who accompanied their husbands came directly from the bush and posed problems for the housing committee. Some of those from the bush had never before seen a flush toilet so that one woman spent all night turning off and on the handle for the real joy of seeing, at long last, enough water! Since many Kikuyu ladies did not know how to handle a knife and fork, the committee in charge tactfully brought their food, bananas, cheese and bread, to their hotel room so that they might not be embarrassed in the public dining room. On the other hand, many of their husbands, delegates who had been educated either in mission schools here or in colleges abroad, with a grasp of world politics and Western ways, spoke into the assembly microphones unconcernedly, both in polished English and in Kikuyu.

One of their knotty issues for recent discussion had been to decide whether or not to baptize a Masai chief and his three wives, who all wished to become Christians. In the old days, the stern rule had been that the chief must get rid of two of his three wives before he could join the church.

"The question is, which two wives shall he cast off?" worried one tall handsome young Kikuyu. "Which children of his own body shall he repudiate? It hardly seems Christian to break up a family in this way. The Masai are a nomadic people; they wander from one grazing spot to another to feed their cattle, which is their tribal wealth, so they have not had the opportunity to hear about Christ that some of the rest of us have had. Many times the Kikuyus and Masai have fought and killed each other over cattle disputes or stolen wives. Is it not up to us Christians to bring peace, not family separation?"

Chief Moses Lemoiko (the applicant for church baptism)

who lived deep in the Masai Reserve, had been appointed chief of his people ten years ago by the British, but so efficient was he and so devoted to the welfare of his tribe that after the Mau Mau "Emergency," his tribe voted to keep him on as leader. Yet when their chief announced that he wished to become a Christian, the Masai, jealous of their own culture and entity, were horrified. The families of his three wives rushed to yank them away from contamination with such a renegade and for a time it looked as if the chief would have no family at all in the four sturdy huts, one built for himself and the others for his three wives and their children, which all clustered on the top of a gentle hill in the Reserve. However, when the news leaked out that most of the chief's trouble had been fomented by another man who wanted to be chief in Lemoiko's stead, the people veered back to the leader known for his justice and tolerance. His wives and children returned to their hilltop homes and the Christian Church crowned this reunion by deciding that the chief and all his three wives might be baptized together.

So the whole family are among the first Christians in the Masai tribe. "The important thing is not what the chief was before, but how he reacted when he came into contact with the gentle philosophy of Jesus Christ," explained one modern missionary preacher. "From now on, he will take no more wives. So within the context of his own culture he will act as a Christian." What does it matter if his adolescent son still has to kill his lion with his spear to prove his manhood? Does this take more courage than the Freedom March of other adolescents in America whose ancestors came also from Africa? Who are jailed, even killed? Chief Moses talks no English but looks intelligently toward the future. He sees that the days of the Masai's nomadic living are numbered, that they must be trained in modern agriculture and in getting along with people of other tribes in the new nation. So he has set aside 1,300 acres for a pilot agricultural training station, and has given the land upon which a small Christian church has been built.

I was curious to meet this man who, though uneducated in the narrow sense of the word, yet was a shrewd, enlightened leader of his people. So on Easter Day, rather than shout Hallelujahs at the great cathedral in Nairobi, I bumped in a small car deep into the bush of the Masai Reserve with the lay leader, half Kikuyu and half Masai, who was to conduct services in Chief Moses' tiny new tin-roofed chapel. We passed many men carrying not only their spears but the polished staffs which indicate that they are on a peaceful mission, not like the younger warriors who carry only their murderous spears. The Masai men are a tall, handsome people who walk as proudly as kings. Legend relates they lived once on the banks of the Nile from which they migrated generations ago. They wear only togalike garments colored with ochre from the red earth, thrown debonairly over one shoulder, with their ears weighed down with bead earrings. One man even wore a watch made of beads. The women were gay in bright-colored single garments but as we passed by them, their shaved heads were frequently bowed almost to the ground by the weight of great water cans, so heavy not even a strong American man can lift them easily. The only car which passed us on the rutted road in a choking cloud of red dust, was a government vehicle which had printed upon its side, "Ministry of Tourists and Wild Life." I wondered if it should not read, "and Other Wild Life."

Curious about the Masai *bomba* with its several thatched huts centered around the circular corral where the cattle are driven each night for safety from marauding lions, I asked our driver if I could see the inside of one of these homes. He obtained permission from his friends and we walked within the thorn bush enclosure. The original Masai hut, made of wood slats bound together with grass and dung-plastered, was so low you had to bend almost double to enter its dark interior, but the newer homes were tall enough inside so I could stand upright; they even had a vent for the smoke of the cooking fire which a young housewife with a beautifully shaped shaven head was tending, poking in twigs to keep the iron kettle gently boiling. She smiled and nodded a welcome in our common language of friendliness. The only furniture was a shelf where the entire family slept at night and a three-legged guest stool. It seemed incredible to me that this quiet homestead could need a guard every night to drive off hungry lions which came down from the harmless-looking tawny hills.

The driver of our car shrugged off my incredulity. "This week, I myself lost twenty-eight cattle. I am a teacher in a little school which has neither doors nor window glass. Yesterday when I arrived with my children, we found a pride of twenty-five inquisitive lions had moved into the classroom before us! The cubs were tumbling and frolicking over my desk where I had arranged the lessons for the day."

"What did you do?" I gasped. "Send for the police?"

"Using what for a telephone?" He explained calmly, "African children know that a loud yell and a big stick are often as good as a spear, so we soon scared off the intruders and the children went back to their books."

I hoped the lions had learned their lesson for at least another twenty-four hours as our car shot away in a cloud of dust so that we should not be late for the Easter service, which fortunately could not begin until the preacher, our driver, arrived. I had been warned that we would have to sit cross-legged upon the dirt floor since the church had no pews. But, to my surprise, rough wooden benches upon which a capacity Easter congregation was sitting filled the little room. Up front was a table where the preacher settled into one chair, and, beside him, as befitted the head of the tribe, sat Chief Moses. Behind their mutual husband, on a bench against the wall, were his three wives in all their bright Easter finery of shukas and beads. Down in front, on the benches where their parents could keep a stern eye upon them, wriggled the assorted offspring, boys in miniature togas or slippery short pants and little girls in short, gay dresses.

Since the service was conducted in Masai, I could not understand what was said, so I watched the congregation which filled the rough benches, women whose cotton dresses tightly outlined their lovely bodies, their beaded earrings pulling down their ears so that the jewelry often touched the wearer's shoulders; young women nursing hungry babies as their mothers sang the hymns; men in togas, who had stacked their spears outside the church door but who sat at the end of the benches in case of sudden emergencies from any attackers; wrinkled old women fingering Bibles they could not read but were learning to recite by heart. Summoned from my back bench to speak about the Fellowship of the Least Coin, I told the friendly Masai through the interpreter, "I bring you greetings from other Christians around the world and ask your prayers for the refugees I am going to meet." Their murmured Masai prayer for my safety was a comforting if invisible spear in my hand; there is nothing more blessed than the greeting of another Christian in a language you may not understand but which speaks clearly to heaven.

As I was introduced to Chief Moses outside the church door later, I inquired through my interpreter, "How did you get the new church benches?"

"They are the gift of the Kikuyu Christians," the chief told me. I stared at him, startled, for only that day I had seen a paragraph in the newspaper stating that yesterday ten Masai and Kikuyu had killed each other in a quarrel over cattle. Chief Moses explained, "The friendly Kikuyu came in a great truck with the benches piled high which they had made themselves for our Easter service. We killed a cow, had a great feast together before they went home."

Truly this was a peace that passed understanding, a portent for the new united Kenyan democracy. If there is any place in the world where the prophecy can be fulfilled that the lion and the lamb may lie down together, it is Kenya. Nature may still be red in tooth and claw, but here even the city dwellers in Nairobi (which has been a sizable city only since 1950) and the animals to whom the bush and forests originally belonged, live in peaceful proximity. Ten minutes by taxi from my sophisticated modern hotel, where the waiter inquired respectfully, "Will you have a demitasse after your dinner, Madame?" lay the forty-mile-long National Game Park, adjacent to the city's modern airport. It surprised no one when one morning an incoming jet was delayed in landing by a lion wandering onto the airport runway. The Kenyans take it for granted that Africa belongs to the animals as well as to them; it is simply a matter of each keeping to his own corner. As the signs read when your taxi drives into the game park . . . DRIVE LEFT FOR LIONS . . . DO NOT HOOT . . . PLEASE DO NOT DISTURB THE ANIMALS.

Safe in your car, you gaze out the open window at a pride of lions, massive golden beasts, male and female, sleepy in the afternoon heat, stretched out in the shadow of a great tree with the two cubs tumbling and cuffing each other. "See the cheetah under that bush?" points out the taxi driver. "He's hard to find because the leaves make shadows so like the markings on his coat. He looks peaceful enough but yesterday one of them took the face off a game keeper who was careless. He would have been killed if his sixteen-year-old son hadn't jumped on the cheetah's back, pulled the cat off his father. Both the boy and his father are doing fine in the hospital. Will you look at those goofy giraffes!"

They had left off nibbling the tops of the nearby acacia trees and, with amazing speed, were loping awkwardly along the horizon like huge children's toys suddenly come to life. Seen close to, their wide shy brown eyes have long lashes like movie stars. On the tawny slopes of the hills fed herds of gazelles, high-leaping impala, and zebra striped like circus tents, as much at home as the little boy I had watched sitting patiently under the Cross beside the Felicia Sunderlal Memorial that morning, waiting for the Fellowship of the Least Coin to fill his little tin pail with milk. In Africa even the wild animals are granted their place in the sun. At least the cheetahs have not yet invented an atomic bomb.

Five

The Least Wanted Children

IF YOU HAD TO WASH four hundred diapers a day in a river that runs by a home for mentally retarded children, would you call this *The Happy Place?* Yet this is exactly what Prithipuri means, the lovely refuge for unwanted children on the sandy seashore with the tall palms waving over the rolling whispering wavelets; on the other side of the jutting point of land lie the calm waters of the river flowing past the several small dormitories and a hospital ward. Here, only a few miles from Colombo, the capital city of Ceylon, live eighty-five mentally retarded boys and girls, including forty-five incontinent, helpless babies, the least wanted children in the entire country. They are sent to the Prithipuri Home by hospitals who no longer have room for them, since they cannot be cured; by police who have picked them up from the roadside or have found them wrapped in newspapers, left in ashcans; or by despairing parents who have spent their last cent trying uselessly to cure their children. But although no one else has room for such waifs, The Happy Place welcomes them, makes for them a real home with laughter and a sunny sea.

This unique experiment in faith is run by a fantastic pair, an English Buddhist monk and a Ceylonese Roman Catholic who used to be a Protestant professor of theology in Northwestern University in Evanston, Illinois.

Reverend Bikku Sumana fifteen years ago gave up his baptized name of William Bates, donned the orange robe and took the begging bowl of the Buddhist monk. His eyes are very blue and twinkling and his bare Anglo-Saxon arm emerging from his garb of Oriental priest is frankly freckled, but he is still the enthusiastic Buddhist who believes that if his faith in the Life Force which is Love is strong enough, everything he or the children in his care need will surely come. The queer thing is that he is right. No matter how disturbed the boy is who is brought to him at Prithipuri nor how dismally hopeless the unwanted baby, he takes them all and the cash for their care comes, miraculously, from the concerned community, from the Fellowship of the Least Coin, and elsewhere.

"We are badly crowded here but somehow we can always make room for one more," he explains, firm in his belief in the eternal goodness of God and of man.

"The children we shelter here are of all faiths, Buddhist, Christian, Moslem, and Hindu," explained the monk as we sat together on the veranda of his tiny home having tea and watching several of his boys playing cricket on the green. "The governing board are equally interfaith. The children, both boys and girls, have only one thing in common; nobody else wants them but us. Some of our older boys are perfectly normal mentally but suffer from emotional disturbances or from conditions in the home which make it impossible for them to stay there. But we go on the modern theory that mentally disturbed children can be helped by living with normal children and vice versa. The abnormal children learn by example to feed themselves, to play as the normal ones do, or even to help in the garden, while the normal children learn patience, understanding, and compassion for those less endowed than they happen to be, mentally and physically. These normal children go to the government school in the village. See that boy over there with the iron braces on his legs and the crutches? He painfully hitches a mile to school every day and back again; he is so determined to get an education, to make a good life for himself as an adult. We encourage this, partly because we have no other way to get him to school and partly because he is developing his muscles of body and mind which he will need greatly later in getting a job."

Dr. Bryan De Kretser, Reverend Sumana's deputy, has as strange a background as the monk himself. He has seen the world and still loves his own small portion best. Born and educated in his home, Ceylon, he received his theological training in the United Theological School at Bangalore, India. He took his doctorate at Edinburgh, Scotland, and taught comparative theology at Northwestern University for some years before returning to Ceylon as pastor of a large Presbyterian Church. At the time when Sumana started his refuge for the mentally retarded children, Dr. De Kretser was chairman of the National Council of Churches in Colombo. However, after the death of his wife, in search of more authoritative spiritual comfort, he became a Roman Catholic. De Kretser decided that works were not only as important as faith but engendered faith itself, so he joined the Buddhist monk in his efforts to care for the children whom nobody wanted at the Prithipuri Home. While connected with the National Council, Dr. De Kretser had been helpful in procuring the lovely point of land between the sea and the river where the mentally retarded children could develop unimpeded as far as was possible for them. Now he moved in to live with Sumana.

These two oddly assorted men, whose over-all imperative was love for people, began their unusual home by adopting two spastic, mentally retarded babies on Christmas Eve. The children's hospital had sent word that they could no longer care for the children.

"It seemed too bad for two babies to be unwanted on the very birthday of the Christ Child so Bryan and I went over to collect them," the monk related to me. His blue eyes, incongruous above his orange monk's robe, twinkled as he added, "Neither of us had ever had anything to do with babies at all so we were rather upset to find that one of them was a girl! However, we had agreed to accept them so we took them back to Prithipuri. We experimented with bottles and nappies and all the rest of it till we learned what pleased small people and what made them howl; so we got along. But then Love sent us help." His tone was as matter-of-fact as if he had said, "We turned on a spiggot and the water came." He went on, "A former nurse who had given up practice because she had had a heart attack came to relieve us of our nursery duties! She has been here ever since. Some of her relatives joined her; twenty-two other volunteers came to help us. Now we care for forty-five such babies and small children in our ward. Would you like to see them? They are Bryan's responsibility. I superintend the older boys and girls from eight to eighteen."

As I followed Dr. De Kretser about his ward, I was too horrified at what I saw to even speak, but he chattered along. "That boy in the bed is sixteen but he looks about six, doesn't he?" Dr. De Kretser remarked. "He is here in the baby ward because he simply lies there, eats, sleeps, and defecates; but he is cared for with love so is happy as he can be. There is no other place in all Ceylon where this can be said, so we feel this work is worthwhile." In the long dreadful (to me) row of small beds were babies with heads almost as large as their bodies, spastic four-year-olds whose legs were so twisted that they were twined around their necks and could not be straightened out, babies with lackluster eyes and gaping mouths . . . I shivered involuntarily but Dr. De Kretser said gravely, "I know what you are thinking—euthanasia. Their bodies are mere vegetables, I grant you, but those children also have souls. When God wants them He will send for them. Life and death stand side by side here and who can tell which is preferable? When one of these small people died in the night recently the nurse in charge washed, prepared him for burial and then calmly went back to sleep till morning. We do what we can with compassion and we leave the rest to God."

All of the workers at Prithipuri are volunteers; no one could possibly be paid enough for doing such work. But a sort of ashram has been formed whereby the workers, two of them unmarried mothers whose children are in the incurable ward, get for their services merely room and board. "And five dollars a month for whatever small things they do not really need," as the Buddhist monk explained.

The Fellowship of the Least Coin has helped by giving money so that these workers may have a rest house where they can sleep and eat in comfort, and where they may enjoy quiet when off-duty. There were neat iron cots with clean folded blankets, a long wooden table with backless benches for their meals, wicker chairs for the rare occasions when they can sit down and rest. Certainly no luxuries but peace and cleanliness. As Reverend Bikku Sumana wrote in his letter of thanks to Mrs. Rathie Selvaratnam, chairman of the Fellowship's Central Committee who happens to live also in Ceylon, "It seems fitting that 'The Least Coins' should be used for the care of 'The Least Wanted Children in Ceylon.' "

The Ceylon Fellowship of Service, "an interracial, inter-religious group devoted to the service of youth" which now manages the affairs of Prithipuri, and which includes, as do the children, Moslems, Hindus, Buddhists, and Christians do not permit proselytizing. The Hindu children celebrate their religious *pujas*, the Moslems are taken to their mosques, and the Christian children who are ambulatory go each Sunday and feast day to the churches of their choice. But sometimes the different groups come to admire some of the practices of other worshipers.

"We Buddhists like to use flowers and candles in our worship and religious acts, and some of the Christian children felt left out when they were not allowed to bring their flowers also," explained Reverend Sumana, his blue eyes following the cricket game in which several mentally retarded boys were playing together with normal boys, a great advance over sitting staring at a wall in a mental hospital. "They wanted to know, 'Why can't we give roses and candles to God too?' The Roman Catholic cardinal here in Colombo heard of their request and he is giving us also a Christian shrine. Of my design," added the Buddhist, chuckling. "It will include a life-size statue of Jesus with three small children at his knee. The inscription will read: 'Suffer the little children to come unto Me.' Here the Christian small people can bring roses also in their worshiping by the river."

The Buddhist monk directs both the work and the recreation of the adolescent mentally retarded boys and girls. Sumana explains, "Many of these youngsters have been shut up in institutions where they have seen nothing except mental sickness; after their contact with normal children, they copy the ways of eating, playing, sleeping. See that little girl over there?" A girl about eight with tangled dark hair and lackluster eyes was lying flat on the concrete veranda with a tin plate of food by her side; as we watched, she reached out languidly, took a handful of rice, ate it and then, seeing us smiling at her, she smiled back. Her face was instantly transformed from lethargy to brightness. The monk said, "Before she came to us, even for months afterward, she never smiled."

"Recently a warden of the lunatic asylum called me to say he had several teenagers, hopelessly retarded, yet whom he did not want to be associated with the older demented men. Would we at Prithipuri take them? I agreed, though I wasn't quite sure what to do with them. Two who acted a bit violent when they arrived I had sleep on the floor with me in my bedroom where I could keep an eye on them. But they proved quite harmless. So one of my helpers volunteered to take these older unteachable boys into a small house of their own, to live with them. Since they are all incontinent we couldn't give them beds! They sleep on the floor and each morning we dump them, blankets and all, into the river! They clean both themselves and their belongings, so they are no trouble." He paused by a gate beyond which I could see half a dozen of these older teenagers with their faces whitened strangely. "They have gotten into the matron's face powder again, I expect," the monk said resignedly. "Well, that does small harm." As he looked at the mixed emotions struggling on my face at the sight of these almost grown men playing at make-believe, for whom there was no release but death, the monk added gently, "Don't grieve too much, my daughter. Think of the worries, the troubles these children of God escape. As long as they are fed, bathed, and loved they are happy here. We do not have to understand these mysteries. All we must do is pray and give."

As I held out my hand to say goodbye, the Reverend Bikku Sumana shook his head and clasped his own thin English hands together. "I am not allowed as a Buddhist monk to touch the hand of a woman," he explained. But his Roman Catholic deputy gave my Episcopalian hand the hearty clasp of friendship. I asked Dr. De Kretser suddenly, "Do you really think that washing four hundred nappies is more rewarding than teaching theology in Evanston?"

He hesitated for a time, for he knew I wanted equal frankness. Then his eyes looked fearlessly into mine. "For me, yes!"

As we drove away along the sandy road by the sea, I pondered how different Prithipuri was from the missions I had known in my childhood, how far this home of mercy was from the psychology of the hymn we used to sing about the poor heathen "where every prospect pleases and only man is vile." For these two, the Buddhist and the Christian on the beautiful island of Ceylon, no child of God was vile.

This modern pragmatic missionary cooperation has very little to do with theological or racial differences. Why is it necessary that every man should worship God in the same way? To give up our special beliefs and ideals would make us as uninteresting, as monotonous as the modern super-highways which run so straight and far that they lull the driver to dangerous sleep. But evil and despair still exist and must be faced. The parable of the man who got rid of one devil, swept and polished his house only to have as guests seven worse devils is as modern as today. To realize there is still a very real miasma of evil one has only to walk down a back street in nearly any city in the world, in New York, London, or Colombo. While keeping to our own beliefs and methods, can we not present a common front to the enemy? An army does not fight with one weapon alone. Guns, tanks, airplanes all have their uses. Are we not discovering an equally diverse armament of the spirit? Jesus did not inquire if the little children he gathered to his side were Jews or Samaritans any more than they care about such differences at Prithipuri, the Happy Place where the Buddhist monk, the Roman Catholic and the Protestant women of the Fellowship of the Least Coin are expressing their compassion for unwanted children.

Rathie Selvaratnam, who lives in Mt. Lavinia just outside Colombo and who is the 1966–1970 elected chairman of the East Asian Central Committee who act as stewards of the Least Coin Fellowship, is a modern woman who is calmly equal to any occasion. I have watched her, poised and elegant in her flowing silk sari, address an audience of several thousand women from many countries, play the organ and piano, sing beautifully, preside over a committee of titled and wealthy women in Colombo debating what they could best do to serve the community. Equally competently, Rathie irons a smooth sari. "Rathie" is short for Rathinavathy, which means "Ruby"; she married a Ceylonese named Selvaratnam—translated as "Precious Jewel." John Selvaratnam, an Anglican priest, is head of St. Thomas's School, which has 1,800 students, mostly Ceylonese but also including boys from the American, Indonesian, and Burmese Embassies, since the school offers some of the highest standards of education in the country. Lessons are taught in Singalese, Tamil, and English, the three languages current in Ceylon. John says of his wife, "I have been married to Rathie for eighteen years but she still surprises me!"

Rathie is a Tamil educated in Singapore, who has behind her a heritage of Christian courage from her early childhood training.

Her father, the Reverend John Handy, was ordained both a deacon and a priest on the day before the Japanese took over Singapore, where he was acting as Deputy Director of Social Services. It was felt important that while the English were interned, he, as an Asian, should be able to continue with Christian baptisms, weddings, and worship. During the occupation, he carried on his religious work, refusing to leave the city, but he sent his family, Rathie, her three sisters, her brother and her mother, back to their former home in Ceylon to wait out the war. The family escaped by night in a ship which was so badly bombed by the enemy that it had to be beached at Sumatra. Many of the terrified passengers leaped overboard into the turbulent waves and were drowned, but under cover of the darkness of that dreadful night, the Handy family managed to get to shore where they hid among the bushes. By some miracle, they got aboard the last troop ship to leave for Java, where with the remainder of their carefully hoarded cash they took a cargo ship back to the safety of Ceylon. They arrived, weary, battered and with only the tattered clothes upon their backs, and took refuge in the primitive house in their former village.

"It was not easy after being brought up with the amenities of our city life in Singapore to adapt to country ways, to open latrines, communal wells, and the rigid rules that governed the conduct of women," Rathie sighs. "The hardest thing was being tied by the local customs, which did not even allow three girls to walk together along the street for fear they would be drawing attention to themselves, advertising, 'We want husbands!' We Handys, used to the freedom between the sexes in the city, found it hard never to be allowed to have even a picnic on the beach with our own boy cousins! I'm afraid we often outraged the village elders by talking and laughing together."

Yet even this lesson was not lost, for she later was able to encourage the African women just emerging from the bush taboos, when they met together in Kampala at the first African Women's Christian Conference, "Twenty years ago we Asian women were just as you are, chattels of the men bound by rigid rules. Up country still in Ceylon, when a man dies, his family has all the say about whatever of her own belongings she shall keep. Unless she hides some of her things with her friends, her husband's family may confiscate them all. The Ceylonese Christian woman of recent years, however, has come into her heritage; she is a person in her own right."

Although most marriages are still arranged by the families in Ceylon, Rathie and John Selvaratnam are partners who chose each other. She gave up her job as principal of St. Hilda's School for Girls in Singapore to which she had gone back after the war, and came home again to Ceylon to marry John in 1950. Instead of a conventional wedding ring, Rathie wears a golden medal on a long golden chain around her neck. The medal is composed of an anchor signifying Faith, a heart for Hope, and cross for Charity, Love. They have three children, Sulochana, the slender young girl who is sixteen, and two sons, Peter and John, eleven and seven respectively. Sulochana was allowed to name her new brother so that she would feel she, too, had a part in welcoming him into the family. She called him "Peter—because *he* was a strong man."

Rathie's mother used to worry because her husband, John Handy, stayed on in Singapore while the rest of them had escaped the occupation. But her husband explained, "The poor laboring people need me even more now that the enemy is here. I have the church also to look after. But I will come to you in Ceylon where I was a boy when and if I feel I am no longer needed here." John Handy did not come home till twenty-five years later; there, although retired at seventy-eight, he still is active as an Anglican priest.

Rathie, who has represented Ceylon at many international gatherings in India, Japan, Europe, Africa, Hong Kong, and the United States, is an imposing woman of great executive ability. She answers some seventy letters a day from all over the world, asking about the Fellowship of the Least Coin. After the race riots in Ceylon between the Singhalese and the Tamils, when many poor Indians were forced to flee to the northern part of the island where they had nothing, no homes, no food, Rathie quietly suggested to the Fellowship that they help the farmers buy some of the farm land which the government was making available so that they could plant vegetables and fruit to feed their hungry families, could cut bamboos to build their own new homes. In this tropical climate where everything grows rapidly, where roofs can be thatched from nearby palm trees, many people were thus fed and sheltered. She has started fifteen Fellowship prayer groups in the island who help to care for Christian workers who have grown too old or too feeble to work longer. She is one of the sponsors of the "matchbox rice gifts" in the public schools.

"This latest plan is to have each school child bring in one matchbox of rice to feed the less fortunate children at Prithipuri," Rathie explains. "It makes quite a job for the teacher of the class because we have so many kinds of rice and each kind must be cooked separately, so the teacher has to keep many matchboxes on her desk. But it is worth it, for the school children are taught sharing with the Prithipuri youngsters. Also, since the work is intercredal, we have a flag day each year, organized by Mrs. Swarma Jayasinghe, when people of all Ceylon buy our tiny flags to raise money to support the 'Least Wanted Children.' "

Ceylon is a country of great social and economic contrasts. People of great wealth who think nothing of installing their own elevator when the owner finds it hard to walk up stairs pass by in their cars. Men in remote rural districts may own nothing except the tiny yellow pleated bag that each wears to protect his vital parts. The most modern jets land at the two airports, yet oxcarts amble along the middle of the country roads delaying the airport bus, making the passenger worry lest he arrive at the runway after his transport leaves. No one except the stranger seems to want to hurry in this lovely languid land. After the abject poverty of Prithipuri, I lunched with gentle Lady Wilfred DeSoysa, who lives in a large gracious home surrounded by jade, crystal, and ivory objets d'art. In her garden she looks out upon some fifty varieties of orchids; but she is proudest of her four sons, one of whom is the Anglican bishop of Ceylon. Her husband, Sir Wilfred, was knighted by Queen Elizabeth for his philanthropic projects and social service, a work which, now that he is ill, Lady DeSoysa herself carries on with great skill. She uses her wealth constructively so that even many not of her faith "rise up to call her blessed." The Christians may be a small minority in Ceylon but they make up in warmth and compassion what they may lack in numbers. One of the greatest joys a stranger can experience, I found, was to mingle with a group of Christians where you understood not a word of what was said, yet felt at home and welcome because you, too, belonged to the Family.

I drove early one morning twenty-five miles from Colombo through the dewy beautiful countryside of this dreamlike island to get to the airport where my V.C. 10, one of the most modern and luxurious jets, was waiting. Our bus passed along the unpaved orange-colored country road, past small thatched houses where mothers were poking twigs under black iron cooking pots for breakfast; where small boys completely naked were tossing stones in a game drawn by a stick upon the ground for lack of any other toys; where businessmen, comfortably waiting for their breakfasts, were sitting on their tiny verandas, reading the morning newspaper, and I thought how alike we housewives were in Sudbury and in this Asian village. A mother dressed only in a sarong came to the open door of her home, smiled down at her naked small son pounding a tin can against the stone doorstep for the sheer love of making a sound he himself had planned; she understood, for she did not stop his racket; she simply laid her hand for an instant upon his dark head and in her touch was all the love in the world. In that instant the Ceylonese mother and I were sisters, for each of us had a beloved son.

Six

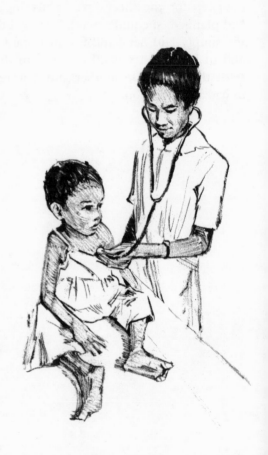

The Young East Goes
Independent

MODERN MISSIONS CAN BE FUN. As a child in a Methodist parsonage, I can recall watching, big-eyed, the packing of the "missionary barrel," which included cast-off corsets for unwary native jungle dwellers as well as worn blankets and winter underwear for the Fiji Islanders. Today, all this nonsense is changed—although doing so must have ended a great deal of hilarity when the barrel was opened at the other end of the journey. I once saw a boy in Fiji using an old-fashioned corset as a swing in a palm tree! Hospitals, social and church workers in various parts of the world requisition whatever is needed or the suitable wants are met, if possible, near the base of operations. Yet when I dropped in by jet recently on ten different countries, attending church in as many languages, I was thrilled by the warmth of Christian *alikeness,* however customs or languages might differ. It was exciting to say the Lord's Prayer quietly in English when everyone else around you was reciting it in Kikuyu or Chinese. It made you remember that the "We Three Kings of Orient Are" about whom you sang in Christmas pageants as a child were real people who had brought different cultures and philosophies to the Manger, then as now. More thrilling was the realization that the journey to find the Christ Child begun so many centuries ago is still going on; *that you yourself are a pilgrim.*

Moreover, even while welcoming you as a fellow Christian, the church in each country has its own customs, its independent spirit, and is bent upon conducting its own missionary efforts by its own methods. No longer is Christianity confused with Mother Hubbards nor are Western forms of worship insisted upon; Bethlehem, Nazareth and Gethsemane belong to worshipers of many faiths and may be visited by modern ecumenical pilgrims filled with wonder at seeing the pages of their Bibles come to life.

I found these very differences stimulating. It was intriguing to kneel in a cathedral pew in Nairobi behind two Scottish men in kilts with the ceremonial dirk peeping out of their long wool socks (or whatever they call them), and to listen to the rich voice of a very black preacher speaking in such a Scottish burr I could barely understand him; to accept a Cross made of two polished sticks presented to me by a boy naked except for a loincloth at a Sunday School in the bush; to be obliged to shake my own hand since the Buddhist monk in Ceylon could not touch a female even though he and the Fellowship of the Least Coin women around the world were all working to care for retarded youngsters; to talk with a young intern from a Thai Theological Seminary who had just returned from working among the aborigines in the river forests who had made it quite clear (politely) that he did not want either help or advice from an American.

The members of the formerly "mission churches" know that they still need financial and technical assistance from Europe and the United States for evangelism and relief work but they want to make use of this help in their own way, thinking, quite rightly, that they understand the psychology of their fellow citizens much better than any outsider possibly can. In a very real sense, there are no more "foreign" missions, only "home" missions. Watching these expanding young churches grow up to meet their own responsibilities is as thrilling as seeing one's own son stand up as an adult to say quietly, "I agree with you in principle, but I do not think that is quite my understanding of this problem." After all, the whole reason for so-called "foreign missions" was to have the man in the pew, whether it be in jungle, bush country, or city, understand "This is *my* Christ, too, and to spread His kingdom is my job as well as yours." The missionary barrel has, I am glad to say, given way to a new humbleness, with the emphasis upon the *spirit* of giving rather than upon charity. The Fellowship of the Least Coin gifts are predicated upon the belief that the recipients in whatever country they may call home are quite capable of administering the Christian program in their own way, of both giving and receiving valuable advice. The recipients welcome this sharing of responsibility, for they know the grant comes from no single source seeking to limit their independence but from women in many nations praying only for their success. There is no quid pro quo involved, as may be true with political or large organizational giving, only concern and cooperation. Youth, especially, everywhere are resentful of supervision by even "their parents in Christ."

The theological students at Chiangmai, for example, decided to form their own Thailand Overseas Missionary Society and to send their graduate students to "intern" among the Ibans, the aborigines of Borneo. These Thai students, it is true, had been trained in Christian schools begun by the West; some of them had been exchange high school or college students in the United States. But they had come to their own conclusion that, wherever it may be situated, "Only a *living* church is any good in the modern world, a church that divides and gives of itself." These "interns" from Chiangmai were familiar with both Eastern and Western thought, but it was as Thais that they went on their own initiative up the deep rivers and into the far valleys of Sarawak to live with the Ibans in their "longhouses."

I happened to attend church service in Bangkok when the leader of this young Thai missionary organization reported to his local sponsors what their representatives had been doing for the past three years in Sarawak. I did not, of course, understand a word of what he was saying, but as I looked around the congregation, I murmured to my American friend, "Three-quarters of these people here are *young!* I never saw so many at a church service!" I stared at the overflowing collection plates, wondering, "Why are *girls* taking up all that money?"

"Because this is the student chairman of the young people's own missionary society who is preaching!" she whispered back. "Mr. Paw Tananan. They sent graduate students to the Ibans and are excited over what this boy is telling them of the life 'back of the beyond.' Sh!"

I understood better why they had been so intent when an older missionary in Manila, whose work is partially supported by the Fellowship of the Least Coin, told me later of his visit to these young volunteers in the wilds of Borneo. He also showed me colored pictures of the jungles and clearings where these boys, Boonrat Buayen and Prayong Muangtha, had been working. How integrated they had become with the native Ibans was shown by the laughter on the face of the small girl who rode piggyback upon one boy's shoulders with her fingers tangled in his hair, while her two-year-old brother leaned casually against the other Thai's knee, with his chubby hand confidingly in the older boy's. These two youthful missionaries might not be blood relatives of the aborigines but it was easy to see that they belonged to the same Christian family.

The older missionary reported: "We went by steamship from the Cibu up the Rajang River, where we transferred to a native long-boat with only an outboard motor. We shot the really terrifying rapids to reach the smaller tributary up which we traveled for days, until we finally came to the villages near the Indonesian border where these two boys had been working alone for three years. They lived in the native 'longhouse,' an apartment house often two blocks in length in which ten to thirty families have their own sleeping quarters but who share the storage facilities for their crops on a wide common veranda, covered to keep out the rain and the thieving animals. Beyond the storage space in the longhouse is also a joint living veranda for the common life of the community where are celebrated weddings and other family festivities. The Thai boys held worship services here also when it was convenient; they fitted into the community life, lived as the Ibans did, explaining their Christian beliefs in words and actions their hosts could understand.

"During their three years there, the Thai boys had made ninety-five converts to Christianity. They organized many small Christian groups along the river banks and had been able, with native help, to build a small thatched church which was filled to capacity on Sunday, for the rivers make good roadways. To animists like the Ibans, life and death are considered to be of one piece; those who have died, those who are still alive, and those as yet unborn are equally members of the same family. The Thai boys explained to me, 'We tried to make the Ibans understand that Jesus Christ is also beyond time and the master of it, that He is Lord of the Dead, the born and unborn, for He has known both life and death which He conquered when he rose at the Resurrection, on Easter morning. Therefore, all eternity is His. To further fit into their tribal background, we used rice in our communion service. To them, rice is almost sacred because their very existence depends upon a good crop. So we selected from among the congregation especially honored servers who should bring offerings of the new rice to the communion table along with the sacred wine. They said, 'This good harvest is not of our own getting; we are only stewards of the soil, joint workers with God. Therefore this good yield of the soil is not ours alone but ours only as stewards. We bring it to the Christian altar to share with those in need who are our brothers.' "

This was the story that those Thai young people, crowded into the hot but exciting service at the Bangkok church that spring morning, were hearing Paw Tananan tell. After the service, he explained to me further in excellent English: "We are grateful for what the older missionaries have taught us; we are not just resentful young Asians wanting to make a go of it on our own! I learned a great deal when I studied in the United States which made it much easier for me to work among philosophies and ways of life different from that of us Thais—just as American ways differ. While each culture expresses its own ideas in art, philosophy and religion, underneath we all as human beings want essentially the same things, a decent life in this world and a belief that there is a God who governs not only today but the hereafter. We all want *some meaning* in what happens to us, some link with the past and with the future. To make Christianity real for the Ibans, whom our boys came truly to love, they saw they would have to make religion tangible to the aborigines in terms they could understand, such as the shared rice on the communion table instead of the traditional bread and wine. This adjustment in no way detracts from the compassionate ideals of the ever-merciful Christ; it merely deepens them, makes them a real part of daily living."

These independent young Christian missionaries of the East, of whom all who have taught them are proud, make the jump to ecumenicity with ease, because tolerance is implicit in their faith. They do not so much defy the centuries-old concept that the woman is a vassal, animated furniture of the home, as ignore it blithely. One hot evening when I attended a meeting of the World Student Christian Federation in Bangkok, I was startled to find an energetic, very attractive Chinese girl in a cheongsam standing up front in the large hall, waving her arms, leading the mixed group in singing energetic college songs. Most of the delegates were boys, students from colleges and universities in Malaya, Hong Kong, Singapore, and Indonesia; the travel expenses of some of the girls present had been paid quietly by the Fellowship of the Least Coin so that girls could take their equal part in student discussions of the special problems of their own countries. Only those who have witnessed the still cowed, burden-heavy woman of many tribes whose body is still not her own, who is bowed under heavy loads of water, fuel for cooking, or mountains of produce, can conceive what a modern miracle this is! But everyone seemed to take it for granted that the lovely clear voice of this girl of the New East should lead all the rest at the Bangkok student conference. Microphones at each table so that the groups could talk easily with each other in the vast room seemed to dismay a few speakers, but most of them took such modern gadgets in their stride.

"The most interesting of these particular students is that handsome boy over there who has become the first Roman Catholic president of the Students' Christian Mission in his home college, a group which was formerly totally Protestant," murmured the student leader at my side. "He's a fireball. He's a senior at the Technical Teachers' College at Kuala Lumpur. When the students of his own creed protested his heading up the group where Protestants would be in the majority and asked him to form a merely Roman Catholic organization at the college, he refused flatly.

" 'In our country where we are a minority, we Christians must all stand together,' he pointed out. 'Most of the students here on campus are Moslems; we Christians are not even allowed to hold our meetings upon the college grounds. Therefore, we must make our stand together, not as Roman Catholics or as different kinds of Protestants. I am staying on as president if they want me to!' "

The other Roman Catholics, convinced, also joined the Kuala Lumpur college group, several of whom had been sent by the World Christian Student Federation as delegates to this convention in Bangkok, where they made their stand for Christ. The sturdy, smiling president said that evening into his microphone, "Even if because of our differing ideas we cannot worship together, we can at least work and talk together as Christians." He grinned. "When I first suggested we invite to our meetings the atheists and Moslems who were making life miserable for us at the College with their threats and interruptions, I was all but shouted down. But we did invite them. After all, what good does it do to always talk only to those who agree with you? To be just a closed cell? Since we allowed the atheists to attend, they listen and are not nearly so aggressive. Who knows? Perhaps we will eventually convince them that we are right."

The Fellowship of the Least Coin figures that to help these coeducational young leaders come together to plan constructively rather than riot in the streets is a worthwhile investment. As I left the meeting that wiltingly hot Bangkok evening, the students from four countries were still singing enthusiastically under the leadership of the pretty Chinese girl in the cheongsam, "This Land is My Land." If these young people succeed in amalgamating the best of many cultures under the Christian flag, we shall have taken a great step forward in preventing future wars. These independent young men and women may build homes which are real democracies, where even adolescents are citizens. As one boy said, "If a family cannot have fun together, they have entirely missed the point of what it means to be a Christian! The Mother Church should understand that we young people are not the arm of the church to be manipulated; we are *ourselves* the church."

"Happy living should be the trademark of the Christian family," agrees Surapol Pooprapand, another young Thai who produces some of the most outstanding radio broadcasts in Bangkok from the studio of the Church of Christ in Thailand. "Our broadcasts have to be like quicksilver, bright and always changing." He added proudly, "Our children's programs have become so popular mothers tell me that on Saturday mornings the children refuse to go outside to play till our hour is over!"

Curious to see how one could combine an ancient Chinese fairytale with Christian ideals, I listened in at the radio control room one Saturday morning in Bangkok to the story of "The Heavenly Spinning Maid and the Cowherd." The story had been dramatized by a young Thai girl and was played by three other young people on the church staff before the microphone. The Chinese tale tells how the Emperor of Heaven wished to reward the Little Spinning Maid for weaving such exciting beautiful material for clothing for the Great Heavenly Ones. He asked the Empress, "What can one give in heaven where everyone is content?" and his wife suggested, "Why not a short stay on earth?"

"Naturally the Little Maid needed a husband to care for and protect her," the story went on with true Asian logic. "Chen-li, a young and handsome cowherd who lived on a tiny farm by a peacock-blue river which runs shouting from the mountains down to the sea, was selected. A fairy cow was sent down to help him and to tell him that a beautiful girl from heaven would soon be bathing in his peacock-blue river." The cow explained to the cowherd, "If you will grab her clothes, she will become your wife." (The story at this point recalled Krishna, the playful Hindu god who swiped the bathing milkmaids' clothes for a lark; probably all ancient tales like that of the great Flood and Noah's Ark have common backgrounds, legends, dim with age, which date back many thousands of years.)

Chen-li followed the fairy cow's advice and he and his Little Spinning Maid lived together happily for several years. Naturally they fell so deeply in love that when the Emperor of Heaven decided it was full time for the Little Maid to return to spin again in heaven, she did not want to leave Chen-li, her dear husband. When she had to obey the summons, the sympathetic fairy cow showed Chen-li how to fly up into the sky after his young wife, but they could not meet, since the Empress of Heaven flung her white scarf between the two lovers. They stretched their hands futilely toward each other across the Milky Way. So the Little Spinning Maid went back to her celestial weaving and Chen-li back to his cows by the peacock-blue river. But the Empress of Heaven, who also loved her Emperor husband was so sorry for them that once a year, on the seventh day of the seventh month, the Little Spinning Maid and the Cowherd appear side by side as two shining first-magnitude stars for a brief reunion in the night sky.*

This gay dramatization was certainly a welcome variation from the "Bang! Bang!" of cowboy guns in many children's programs I had watched in the United States where violence seems to have become essential juvenile entertainment. The Bangkok radio producer ended the drama by remarking, "God knows what is best for us all; we may think we know best but He knows better. In Ecclesiastes 6:12 in the Christian Bible we read: 'For who knoweth what is good for a man in his life, all the days of his life which he spendeth as a shadow?'" The broadcaster answered his own query with the comforting warmth, "Jesus Christ knows and cares for little children."

"What's the use of preaching always to listeners who are already Christian? Except to encourage them now and then," asks Surapol, as impatient of slower yesterdays as the Malaysian student. This slender young Thai executive has a quick smile and an alert, restless mind always searching for new ways to improve on today's methods of communication. Since from ten to twenty percent of his financial support from the West is being withdrawn yearly, he realizes, undismayed, that he will have to depend more and more not only upon his own ability to make money, but upon the pull of better

* Story dramatized from *Chinese Fairy Tales* by Leslie Bonnet, published by Frederick Muller, Ltd., London, 1958.

broadcasts and tapes for his audience. "In a tragic, confused world, the church has to sell itself anew, to prove its sincerity by action," Surapol insists earnestly. His modern church program has captured one of the largest radio audiences in the capital city of Thailand.

"Our programs are aimed at helping to solve neighborhood problems," explained Surapol when I visited him and his crew, young people under thirty, at the church broadcasting studio. "We announce who we are. Then we show our concern for the whole community, over ninety percent of whom are Buddhist, by advising how to avoid cholera by boiling the water that is taken from the klongs or canals. Or (like Dear Abby) we discuss the family worry over how to deal with today's restless teenagers. The revolt of youth is nothing new. Bible dramas can be made as exciting for the average young listener as Westerns: in the end the good guy wins. The flooding energy of the idealistic teenager can be channeled into practical good will projects through modern media, like radio. And our stories come from the East. Jesus himself was a 'rebel' at only twelve; he worried his parents by staying behind to have 'a bull session' at the temple."

Surapol is entitled to put "Reverend" in front of his name but he seldom does, since he considers that "the layman should be as much a priest as the man in the pulpit. The apostles were fishermen, everyday people who knew how to fish, to make tents, who lived their religion on the job. Everyday theology, the discussion of what God wants for our lives, should be as much a part of our business day as the on-the-road conversation with the fellow traveler to Emmaus, not a monologue to be broadcast by the preacher 'only on Sunday.' " Surapol, who is certainly a member of the "Now Generation," is a prominent graduate of the Bangkok Christian College, which has such high scholastic standing that it could easily double its student body of two thousand boys; he has also studied theology at Burma Divinity School in Rangoon and at Chiangmai University in northern Thailand. But he prefers to let the Old and New Testaments speak directly to his radio audience.

"When we offered over the air to give free Bibles to our listeners, we had over eight thousand telegram and letter requests backlogged," he told me. "The Fellowship of the Least Coin helped by sending us enough cash to buy four hundred Bibles to mail to those who most wanted to read them. One young couple wrote: 'We have just been married and wish to build our lives together on this rock.' Another rather desperate letter came from a chap who explained, 'I have been chosen deacon of my church but I am most unhappy since many of the pages are missing from the Bible which I inherited.'"

"The Blue Dove" is another practical answer to a prayer in which the international Fellowship acted as agents. This station wagon, equipped with a projector, tapes and screen, serves school children as well as villagers. Religious instruction is allowed weekly in the Thai public schools but since few of the teachers are Christians, and most Buddhists are unfamiliar with Bible stories, tapes relating the exciting drama of David and Goliath or the miracle when a small boy's lunch of loaves and fishes fed five thousand, are sent to those schools who ask for them. To the Easterner, steeped in mysticism, miracles have been commonplace for thousands of years, are as tangible as rice.

The Reverend Melchizedek Solis, the first missionary co-worker in Thailand from the Philippines, had prayed wistfully for a car equipped with a small picture screen and a projector. There was nothing in his limited budget to allow for such a car but he went on praying. One morning Solis looked out to find parked directly in front of his office the answer—a jeep! It looked a bit battered but still usable. A doctor from a Christian hospital one thousand miles to the north of Bangkok came into the church center's office to explain he wanted only to borrow a wrench so he could patch together the jeep in order to turn it in on a new one. A jeep for sale and cheap! Desperately Mr. Solis took a chance on offering the doctor a very low purchase price, explaining how he hoped to use the car.

The doctor, another Filipino who had come to Thailand as a fraternal Asian worker, impulsively tossed Solis the car keys, saying, "For such a need, I will give the jeep to you, *free!*"

The jeep proved too expensive to run because of its age, but it made a good down payment on a new station wagon not too wide to go through the narrow side and village streets. The Fellowship of the Least Coin quietly added $1,000 for purchasing the new car and the remainder was provided by the local church members. So The Blue Dove (as the Reverend Solis named the sky-colored miracle car) flitted off at last over the countryside, showing films on its own screen to thrilled audiences in the villages. Similar films are sent all over the country, on request, for use even by the universities.

The Blue Dove flies again under the aegis of Surapol Pooprapand, who, young businessman that he is, also uses The Dove indirectly to pay for his radio broadcasts. Since he found he had to hire a crack mechanic to service his audio-visual projects, Surapol arranged for the same mechanic in his spare time to repair all kinds of electrical equipment for his radio audience. Excellent Christian service with batteries and tubes has resulted in about a thousand dollars a year's extra income—a good business as well as good broadcasts.

Surapol and his attractive young wife live in an apartment up two steep flights of stairs in the Christian Community Center in Bangkok where, in spite of having a five-months-old baby, she manages to teach the smaller children's classes. The three-year-old son folds his small hands gravely in the polite Thai greeting when strangers come to interview his father, who is one of the busiest young men in the city. The community radio programs he has been putting on have so interested the new and more powerful shortwave radio station being built in Manila to serve all Southeast Asia with its three frequencies that Surapol has been asked to prepare a test series of programs suitable not only for Thailand but for Laos and the Philippines.

"This would include two hours every afternoon and two hours at night," Surapol explained, his face lighting up with the enthusiasm of creative planning. "For the afternoons, I shall offer one hour of Bible drama, beginning perhaps with Daniel in the lions' den with, of course, realistic sound effects." He smiled engagingly at his own small enchanting son, as respectfully motionless as a delicate carved figure on the mantlepiece. "The other hour will be news and music from many countries, which speaks an international language to young and old—not only hymns and classical music but jazz and the Beatles. In the evenings, we will offer study classes. Most Laotians have not gone beyond the fourth grade in school, certainly not beyond the seventh grade. As adults they want to learn at night to prepare for better-paying jobs. We plan to teach by radio, geography, science, and English. We will mimeograph the lessons which the listeners may send for if they like; we will check the answers and return them. Anyone can learn who wants to, of course, but he will know that the course is church-sponsored. The Christian missionaries started many of our schools here originally; we are merely going a step further giving adult education over the air in the modern way."

So independent have these young people in the Christian Church in Thailand become that twenty young men have asked the Least Coin Fellowship to sponsor their going to Vietnam, not to fight with guns but to offer compassion. They want to work with the village people burned out of their homes or driven from their rice fields by the war, to show that Asian Christians really care what happens to them, no matter what their creed. The Fellowship of the Least Coin were also rather set back on their heels by being asked by a Vietnamese Buddhist woman if she could not join the fellowship of prayer. She was welcomed to contribute her prayer and her small coin to be distributed by Christian women everywhere. One Thai college student explained, "Formerly the most important unit in Asia was the family, including even the distant members. In a way, it is bad that these ties are breaking down; but the positive side of the situation is that the Christian family in Asia and Africa is now being enlarged to take in all people, whatever their tribe or belief."

Asian Christian women have had a large part in giving an international flavor to the efforts of the native church. Mrs. Jannuan Suriyakham of Lampang, Thailand, a former chairman of the Fellowship of the Least Coin Central Committee, has long been working among the thousands of Protestant women in her country. She has also found time from raising a family of five lively children to go to the United States to explain her country's needs and ambitions to the Western world. Accustomed to the crisp voices and decided opinions of many New York and Washington executives and newspaper women, it was a pleasant surprise to me to find that this Thai woman could accomplish just as much with her gentle voice and Oriental courtesy.

Jannuan is a dark-haired friendly woman with delicate ivory features, yet there is a note of authority when she speaks that kept in line even the excited carload of adolescents with whom she and I rode out to a youth conference. Instead of throwing up her hands like so many American mothers today, saying apologetically, "You know how kids are these days!", she took part in the laughter but she never permitted the group to get raucous. Perhaps an inner calm is contagious. Married over thirty years ago to a doctor of medicine, Jannuan has been necessarily much alone. Her third child was only a few months old when her husband left for two years of additional medical training at Tulane

University. Today he is a very successful doctor with his own clinic at Lampang, from which Jannuan traveled several hours to Bangkok in order to explain to me the special problems of the Christian Church in Thailand and what the Fellowship of the Least Coin has been doing to help solve them, such as contributing to the purchase of the Blue Dove, giving immediate relief to refugees made homeless by a hurricane.

"My husband makes a good living but we are not wealthy because to put five children through college these days is quite a squeeze," Jannuan smiled. "But I am proud of them all, not only because they have interesting jobs but because they are international in their outlook. The father of the grandson whose fourth birthday I am helping to celebrate here this week in Bangkok is with the Thai Oil Company; one of the girls is an expert accountant; another is a field worker for SEATO. Our youngest daughter, who has just graduated from Chiangmai, has been granted a fellowship to study mass communication in England. Another daughter with two grandchildren is married to a hydraulic engineer, half Chinese and half Filipino, who teaches at the University of Pittsburgh."

This ability to adapt to many cultures is partly due to the natural graciousness and shy friendliness of the free Thai people, who have never been a colony of any Western nation: they have no need to throw their weight around to prove to themselves or to others that they are the equals of anyone. But the poise of the Suriyakham children certainly owes much to the wise training in their own home.

Jannuan herself is a graduate of the Wattana High School in Bangkok; she is better educated than many women with college degrees, for she has been around the world to see what most students only read about in books. In 1953 she was a member of one of the first Fellowship Teams sent by the Presbyterian Church from Thailand to get acquainted with other Christian women in the Philippines, Hong Kong,

Pakistan, and India where Jannuan and Shanti Solomon met and at once became close friends. In the same year that Shanti was pondering the need of a world prayer fellowship of women, Jannuan was selected by the Smithsonian Institution to be the Thai representative on a team of Asian women from nine countries who were to tour the entire United States to inspect our social service, agricultural, and public health work. Jannuan arranged for her eldest sister to come to Lampang to take care of her growing family while she discovered the United States and they discovered her.

"I have no idea why I was chosen; it just came out of the blue," she says modestly, forgetting her already outstanding leadership among women in her native country. "We flew first-class to New York, but I didn't like this as much as going coach with other people. It's too lonely. We went to see the lovely white city of Washington and then across country, visiting both city and country slums, from Harlem on the East Coast to the West Coast migrant workers. We visited homes of middle-class people like ourselves and also the farms to find out what kind of fertilizer and modern machinery were most efficient for us, too. We were asked to talk at the public schools along the way to tell of our own country to the American children. After I had finished in one classroom telling about the needs of some of our less fortunate Thai children, a small boy of nine came up and thrust a folded paper into my hand."

"You can use this any way you like. For your people," the boy told Jannuan gravely. "It's my allowance for this week." After the boy left, she opened the paper to find a fifty-cent piece.

She kept the coin to show to her own people the real concern of even an American nine-year-old when, back home in Thailand, she went from village to village explaining modern methods of hygiene, farming, and child care which she had learned in the States. "I found the same yearning

East and West," she said. "Everybody's lonely till we meet in
Christ."

From this point of view to the international prayerful
concept of the Fellowship of the Least Coin was only a hop,
skip, and a jump. Jannuan was sent as a delegate to the first
Asian Church Women's Conference at Hong Kong, where it
was decided that if the Least Coins came from all over the
world, they should be also used for the needs of all six continents. At the second Asian Women's Conference, held four
years later in Petchburi, Thailand, and attended by eighty
women from sixteen countries, Jannuan was elected chairman
of the Central Committee of the East Asia Christian Conference, who act as stewards for allocating the Fellowship's
funds everywhere. What each country gives is never announced; the gifts come from the women of the world to
go back to the world.

A bad hurricane had wrecked South Thailand just before
the international delegates arrived at Petchburi. Whole villages had been wiped out, making three thousand people
homeless, and the newspapers showed gruesome pictures of
a woman cut in two by a fallen tree, of dead and mangled
children. The conference at once voted $5,000 for immediate
relief from the Fellowship of the Least Coin fund and the
local Church of Christ doubled this amount. "The minister
of the interior who gratefully accepted the gift seemed some-
what stunned because he had never heard of the Fellowship,"
Mrs. Suriyakham chuckled. "But he appreciated the help. It
bought two hundred mosquito nets, many blankets, and
medicines. It is this swift gift from the heart that makes
the Fellowship giving important; for it is not so much *how
much* you give, but *how* you give it that makes people proud
to receive as well as you proud to give."

The understanding and tolerance that grew among women
of many nations at this Petchburi meeting convinced the
Fellowship of the Least Coin that similar person-to-person
contacts were important to build world peace and Christian

cooperation. Therefore the way of delegates whose native churches could not afford to pay their fare, were paid by the Fellowship to Tokyo in 1966 to the Third Asian Church Women's Conference, where nineteen different countries were guests of the Japanese. Among the newcomers were two from Africa, two from Lebanon, and two from Indonesia. One of the Thai delegates who returned home by way of India and visited famine-struck villages, told Shanti, wide-eyed, "I thought we were poor in our country, but I never realized what a desperate thing it is to be really starving till I saw some of those mothers holding their skeleton babies. It is one thing to hear about big-bellied starving children, even to see them on TV; it is quite another to watch a friend snatch at food like an animal."

Such vivid on-the-spot meetings bring home to both giver and recipient not only their human alikeness but their sisterhood in the family of Almighty God. Jannuan murmured, "When a small boy in America can give away his week's allowance just because he has met a strange lady from another country, the gift does something good to him; he will carry tolerance with him all his life." Meeting with these dedicated Christian women in many countries gave me both humility and pride in just being a woman!

Seven

Tourist in Vietnam

WHEN I TOLD MY EDITOR in New York that as an American tourist I didn't need a visa to stay in Vietnam for a week to see the relief work which the Asian Christian churches and the Fellowship of the Least Coin were doing, he exploded, "What kind of a crazy war is this? Tourists welcome!"

"Crazy war" is right. Almost anything anyone says about what goes on there can be true, conditions vary so from place to place and from day to night, one might almost say, from hour to hour. The only permanent thing is the cloud of uneasy tension that hangs over Saigon, that city of often quiet-seeming streets where pretty school girls in gauzy ao-dais ride motorcycles with their white dress panels floating out behind them, small boys carry their bags of school books or try to sell you a newspaper at three times its price, yet where death may ride in any taxi and a bomb be lobbed into the restaurant, bar, or crowded street corner upon which you stand. Saigon at war is like the entrance to a vast theatre with the twisted mask of comedy on one side of the door and that of utter tragedy on the other. The joker in the tourist deal is, of course, that few sightseers want to fly into Tan Son Nhut airport, where the civilian planes can land only by day, after the military have checked out the snipers. No taxis are allowed in the airport any more, so the traveler has to be met by friends with a permit to enter.

127

"Hello! Nice to see you again." Jim Atkinson, the tall Englishman whom I had last seen at relief headquarters in Hong Kong, held out a welcoming hand as he explained, "I've been loaned here for a while to help U Thaung Tin, who's head of Asian Christian Relief in Vietnam. Our bus is right over here."

There seemed to be war not only on the battlefields but in the Saigon street traffic, fighting for the right of way. Besides the military and civilian cars, hundreds of brightly painted motorcycles and bicycles with noisy motors, apparently just off the assembly line, jostled, honked and sped in all directions like aimless water bugs on a pond. Some carried whole families including the husband, wife and three babies; one driver so small he could barely see over the handlebars and looked about ten years old, cut so closely in front of our bus the driver had to slam on the brakes. When I asked, astonished, how so many supposedly poverty-stricken Vietnamese could afford so many brand-new machines, Jim shrugged. "Black market, I suppose. War jobs. They 'never had it so good.' "

The Vietnamese have been fighting someone (if only each other) for twenty-eight years, long before most of these riders were born, I thought. Why save money? Why not spend it on something shiny, fast, and satisfying for the only safe moment you were sure of? My hotel overlooking the Saigon River with its endless water traffic had armed, bored guards at the entrance, but the open-air bar was doing a rushing business with glasses clinking with real ice in both hard and soft drinks, welcome in the hot humid air. *Hope,* the huge white hospital ship, was tied up at its landing across the street from the hotel, but no patient was visible on its decks, while, beyond, the freighters glided sluggishly up toward the docks; busy little patrol boats with the lookouts on each bow were passing and repassing, watching for camouflaged floating mines.

"Tonight our government and the Viet Cong will fight it

out across on the other side of the river, with the big guns,"
the desk clerk told me in French. "Tough black marketeers
snipe there, too. You'd better keep your wooden shutters
closed in your room. Boy!" He handed my bag to a lad in a
white suit, not much bigger than the suitcase, who led me
what seemed a couple of blocks down a long dark corridor
where small brown men in white uniforms squatted every
twenty feet or so. The boy explained, "Room boys watch
for thieves." I could see why when I tried to bolt my bedroom door and the lock came off in my hand; the screws had
been removed, then lightly shoved back into place. I might
as well be squatting in that corridor myself for all the privacy
I had attained. How did I know which (if any) of those
watchers came from Hanoi? They all looked exactly alike.
My door bursting open made my heart skip a beat but it
was only the room boy with fresh towels.

"You desire a beer?" he asked. "Very cold?"

"No. I'd like some bottled water to brush my teeth," I
told him. Water in Asia was apt to have a lot of bugs for
Westerners, and I hadn't time to get sick here.

I explored the bathroom to find there was no tub, only
a shower with two pipes, one marked "Hot" and the other
"Cold" but never the twain did meet. You took your choice
of being boiled or frozen. The room boy was back with his
bottle of beer. "More safe than water," he insisted but we
finally settled for hot tea. As I drank it, I remembered the
list I had been shown of Civilian Overseas Church Personnel
with one chilling notation, "Gerber, Daniel. American. Place
of Assignment Unknown. Abducted by VC's May, 1962."

The homely companionable sound of the phone ringing
by my hard clean bed was welcome.

"Would you like to go to Cai Be tomorrow?" Tommy's
voice asked. "Tommy," as all his friends call him affection-
ately, is U Thaung Tin, the dignified, efficient head of Asian
Christian Relief since 1965 when it was inaugurated by the
East Asia Christian Conference. He comes from Burma as

does his delightfully curved, smiling, elegantly dressed little wife who looks as if she had never had to lift a hand in her life but who runs the billet where she manages meals and rooms for a dozen international workers and visitors. They drop in from all corners of the earth, may stay a few days or perhaps weeks if the houses for the workers in the relief camps are not ready yet for them.

"Dr. Whitehall and his wife from Australia are going down to inspect how best to put in a water supply in the house where they are to live," Tommy explained. "And there's a barracks there that may be used for a temporary hospital." Cai Be was seventy miles south of Saigon on the Mekong Delta, but the car would not call for me before eight-thirty in the morning because civilian traffic had to wait till the military had cleared off the mines laid by the VC during the night.

"Mines?" I suggested, "Why not make it nine a.m.?"

Tommy, ignoring my dubious levity, said that this main road had been opened as "safe" (at your own risk, of course) for only six weeks, but the Asian Relief had been down to Cai Be several times. Some 15,000 refugees, burnt out of their own houses by napalm bombs or driven out by the VC terrorism, the very people I had come to see, lived along this road in small settlements built by the South Vietnamese government with USAID help. There was, as yet, no resident doctor available for them though several cases of cholera and bubonic plague had appeared, so the Australians were being sent as a team to Cai Be. If I didn't want to go . . .

"Of course I'll go," I told him. "How do the Fellowship of the Least Coin help you?"

"The ladies bought part of the first tons of rice we brought in to feed the starving Montagnards, the mountain people. They gave also for children at Tuy Hoa refugee camp and for building an all-Vietnamese Evangelical church in the suburbs of Saigon—I'll tell you later. The bus will call for you tomorrow."

This war got crazier and crazier—a "safe road" which the VC's mined every night and we un-mined every morning. As the big guns across the river shook my bed all night, I closed the shutters, tried to sleep in my room with no real lock on the door. About half of the population of Vietnam lived on the Mekong Delta, including the thousands of re-housed refugees I was to see. It was important to take this rich rice bowl of the country out of VC control. How could a city so quiet-looking in the daytime be so noisy at night? Why was anyone foolish enough to come to a war as a tourist? Turn over and go to sleep. The bus will be here at eight-thirty.

Dr. John Whitehall from Chester Hill, Australia, was driving with his wife, Elsie, a former kindergarten teacher, on the front seat; they sat me between them. Both were in their early twenties. She was blonde with a gay little pony tail, and slender tanned legs, while he looked as darkly handsome as a TV actor, but he must know his business, since he'd been resident at Sydney Hospital last year. They'd both volunteered for this dangerous, almost impossible job of caring for the health of nearly 200,000 people including, besides the refugees, the rapidly growing town of Cai Be. It was a good thing the Whitehalls were both young and sturdy; he drove the bus with adventurous abandon over patched-up shell holes in the macadam and creaking temporary river bridges where spotters with rifles stood at each bank ready to sink mines floating in the water. I had not realized before that Australia and New Zealand were actually working members of the East Asia Christian Conference; racially they were so different from my other Asian friends, but geographically they did belong to the East. Working side by side was the best way for such Christians to really get to understand each other. U Thaung Tin with his calm Burmese maturity made a good boss for these seventeen eager young people on his two relief teams, one already working at Tuy Hoa and the new one to be stationed at Cai Be.

Traffic was heavy on the road down the Delta but I noticed that no car seemed to want to get off the macadam. About every 200 yards were parked half-tracks bristling with South Vietnamese soldiers, and every so often a big gun stood waiting and watching for trouble. Army trucks are large and have to be catered to, and the civilian buses, crowded to the open windows, drove so close it seemed as if we would scratch off each other's car paint. Once when collision seemed imminent, I closed my eyes and the young doctor laughed.

"They're afraid that 'the soft shoulders,' as you Americans call them, may be still mined. Not that it matters much, since most are not contact mines. See those workers down in the rice fields over there?" Small brown men dressed only in black shorts, with the sun beating down upon their bare backs, were bending over in the rice fields on either side of the road, or were fishing in the deep irrigation ditches. Or seemed to be fishing. It further adds to the confusion of this crazy war that it is impossible to tell the "Wogs" from the "Slopes" as the GI's call North and South Vietnamese. The doctor explained that the VC put almost invisible wire across the road, attached to the mines. "When they see something passing that riles them, the VC simply pull the wire to set off the mine. Last time I drove down here, a whole busload of civilians were blown to bits shortly after I went by. Maybe someone hadn't been giving enough rice to the hungry VC."

Even if it did say *Asian Christian Relief* on the side of our gray bus, anyone had only to look through the car windows to see that most of us were white Westerners. As we crossed a makeshift bridge where the former supports had been twisted into fantastic circles of steel, I murmured, "Maybe it's a good thing we have a doctor with us. I wouldn't care to be minus an arm or leg."

He said soothingly, "Don't worry. The big bang would be curtains."

We were now really out in the open country. Lining the

road were the thousands of tiny new houses of bamboo and thatched reed put up for the refugee farmers and their families. Around each hut was a carefully dug muddy ditch where ducks swam and quacked. "They're most useful for food, for the feathers used in pillows, and the bones are ground up to feed the hogs," the interpreter in our bus explained. Some of the new settlers had already begun to raise gardens in the rich Delta soil, and a few even had trained up morning glories or other flowering vines to decorate fronts of their houses. The women and children came running out to inspect us, to smile and to talk to us through the interpreter. When the young doctor spotted a mother with a plump baby, he slammed on the car brakes, took out his camera, asked, "Take picture, please?"

The mother was delighted, for she knew she'd probably get paid a coin; even the baby on her arm was so excited he let go from his bare undiapered bottom. The mother calmly reached down, dipped his rear end in the muddy ditch, then held him up dripping for the picture. "Do they drink that ditch water?" I wondered.

"Why not? They drink such water since babies," the interpreter answered. "Those big jars up on their verandas are to catch rain water." The doctor snapped shut his camera, remarked that probably they were already pretty immune to most bugs, but his wife said firmly that she wanted a well at Cai Be with a cover on it and water piped into their house. "Yes, dear," he agreed absently like any other well-brought-up husband.

"Well, the clinic will need it and so will I if I'm to work with kindergarten children," she insisted.

Suddenly a roar of helicopters swept over the road like a mighty wind; truckloads of South Vietnamese soldiers seemed to spring from nowhere, crowding our bus to the soft shoulders of the road; jeeps full of dusty Americans in hard battle hats rattled by. As we looked, startled, down a side road across the rice fields we saw more ammunition carriers, tanks, more and more soldiers . . . "Something's up, it looks like," commented Jim Atkinson dryly. "Maybe we'd better check in with the major at the Command Post down the road."

Headquarters certainly sounded a lot safer than parking on a possible mine by the side of a road full of rushing troop transports, looking out at clouds of black and white smoke from a battle going full blast just beyond the rice fields. The small Command Post was of sturdy concrete with sandbags piled around the lookout. As we went inside, carrying our lunch baskets and the Cokes we'd brought for the American boys, the radio was clamoring loudly, "The animal is already up as far as 47!" An American boy with no shirt on in the dripping heat, so you couldn't tell his rank, but wearing thick trousers and GI boots against the snakes that infest the Delta, was putting up small flags on the large map of the vicinity upon the wall.

"Come in! But the major's not here. He's kinda busy," the American soldier greeted our motley crew of men, a woman, and a pretty girl carrying picnic baskets into a battle area. "We're fighting Operation Cedar Falls, the biggest push we've made yet in the Mekong Delta." He listened to the chattering radio while he shifted the battle flags that told where our side and their side were on the map. "We got them pretty well hemmed in here up in the northwest sector—we think," the mapper soothed. (It seemed to me rather silly for the radio to yell about "the animal" when both sides knew whom was meant, but orders were orders.) "If we can wipe out that stronghold, the road can be made permanently safe—safer," he corrected.

It gave you an eerie feeling to be at the focus of a battle only a few miles away that you couldn't see or do anything about, to know that where those small flags went up were men killing each other while you sat in safety among sandwiches and ginger ale bottles. The unbelievable scene gave me the same nightmare feeling of unreality as watching the

"moment of truth" in a bull fight in Spain when the matador
knows that the deftness of his final short sword will mean
death to the animal, or his failure, a vicious goring for
himself. Only here in Vietnam there would be no applause,
no prized bull's ears for the winner, just the satisfaction of
going on living for a few more hours.

"Where you from, ma'am?" asked one of the sweaty American boys politely. "Boston's a long way from my home. I
live in the state the best president of the United States we
ever had came from—Missouri. You wanna see how we make
out here at the post? It's not so bad as the barracks for the
South Vietnamese next door."

The bedroom with its heavy gray concrete walls brightened by the usual girly pictures had four Army cots and out
beyond was the place where the soldier suggested delicately
I "might like to wash your hands." There was a proper
toilet seat but I couldn't lift the heavy milkcan filled with
water to flush it. But what they were proudest of was the
water filter machine, that worked when the electricity did,
infrequently. The eager boy host offered, "Have a drink of
real good water? They put some stuff in it here but we don't
trust it; we use this machine. It's quite safe." I tried to forget
the muddy ditch, the quacking ducks and the baby's dripping
bottom as I held out my hand for the glass, for it was impossible to refuse him. The boy was right; the water was
fine if tepid.

"Have some sandwiches?" the doctor's wife invited him
in return but he said they'd eat later when the push was
over. The radio went on clattering as we ate our lunch on
the missing fighting major's long wooden table. I asked the
GI near me, "Do you think we can possibly win, when
every night the VC undo what we did the day before? Or
even win the 'psychological war' by giving these poor
bombed-out refugees new houses, ducks and schools? I saw a
lot of children on the way up here with US plastic school
bags of books."

"Well, I dunno," he said cautiously. "If we could really
take control instead of just being 'advisors' we might do the
refugees more good. What gets me all hot and bothered is
the way someone up at Saigon steals the food and medicines
before they get here to the villagers. I'm the medic here.
Last week, when bubonic plague broke out among the newer
refugees, we were supplied with antitoxin and disposable
hypo needles to inoculate thousands of 'em. I was so busy
stickin' howlin' kids I didn't look up for some time and then
I yelled to my South Vietnamese counterpart who was doin'
the same job across the room, 'Hey, you're supposed to use
a new needle for each patient!' He yelled back, 'I can't. I
only got enough needles to change at every two hundred!'
Some black marketeer musta swiped his needles. He knew
as well as I did that he might be passing on hepatitis, almost
any kind of bug, if the patient he was sticking happened to
have it. What I can't understand is folks being mean enough
to swipe food and black plague medicine *from their own
people!"*

I stared aghast. "But surely the U.S., the Saigon government send enough food for the refugees to eat properly?"

Jim Atkinson reproved me, "Don't put the poor chap on
the spot. He's in the Army now. Food, aid, medicines go into
the funnel, enough for everyone, but somehow only a trickle
comes out the other end." He added defensively, "When
you've lived in the East as long as I have you'll know a certain amount of pilferage is expected."

I said hotly, "I don't call it by such a polite name when
it concerns bubonic plague! If we've got half a million American soldiers here, and heaven only knows how many civilian
workers, why don't we stop the 'pilfering'? Especially from
the refugees who have nothing and need everything?"

"If you knew the answer you'd be a general at least." The
medic sighed. Then his face brightened into a broad grin.

"You know something? I'm leavin' for home in four months, two days and three hours!"

"That's wonderful," I agreed, watching the sweat make little dirty rivulets down his bare stomach. To me this damp heat was a worse enemy than the VC. I tried to think of something cheerful to say to this homesick boy. "Most of these refugee homes we passed on the way down the road looked better than the old beat-up farmhouses further back in the country. And these new places do have water for gardens and ducks."

The American boy said, *"But it isn't really home!"*

Home was where the heart was, where your roots were even if the house had been burned down and your rice crops had been stolen; or if you came from Missouri.

Later I sat on the front car seat, wiping the sweat out of my eyes so I could see, as we drove on down the now quiet Delta road to Cai Be proper. Many of the farms of these displaced villagers living here were only a few kilometers away, back country, but they couldn't return to harvest the crops without risking their lives. Saigon government sympathizers were constantly being kidnaped, shot, their mutilated bodies thrown aside as a warning. Some advocate that we Americans should be as tough as the Vietcong, that this is the only kind of fighting they respect and fear; that if they cut out the tongue of one of our boys, we should do the same to one of the VC prisoners, hang up his gaping jaws for all to see. What, then, are we fighting for? To beget horror with horror? Or as a so-called Christian democracy to insist upon the right of all people to govern themselves as they see fit? War is an anachronism in a nuclear world where an entire nation can be wiped out in a matter of minutes. Our scientific know-how and common sense *has* to find some other way of settling international disputes. Maybe the Fellowship of the Least Coin are not mere impractical idealists to trust instead in the power of prayer, in the long-term teaching of a new generation that

killing doesn't settle international disputes, merely postpones
the next war, till enough tanks, guns, and planes can be built.
Prayer is in action in cities and villages all over the world
where women are saving their small coins to send doctors
and nurses to Cai Be and Tuy Hua, to cure pain and to
teach hygiene, to send lost children kindergarten teachers
who show them how to play again. There has to be some
end to this mad cycle of killing and being killed, to the "detention camps" with barbed wire and thorn fences that the
Nairobi women had also known so well. Might not this
great fellowship of prayer, secret and sincere, be a small step
toward outlawing senseless violence? Is there any better answer? A Man died to prove that love is stronger than hate or
death; He is still so important that even secular history dates
from His birth. We have to go on trying in His name.

As we drove up the blistering hot dusty road to the house
at Cai Be where Dr. Whitehall and his Elsie were to live,
the walls looked cool and thick. The two rooms downstairs
had been freshened with light-blue paint; there was even a
small locked case with a bottle of iodine, some aspirin and
cotton inside, hardly adequate to treat two hundred thousand
patients! A cage of guinea pigs cluttered the backyard which
smelled so loudly of the filthy river or canal behind it, you
hated to breathe. Around the door, curious children pushed
each other aside to eye the new Americans. The heat was so
intense even young Elsie Whitehall looked pale as she fanned
herself after climbing the ladder to the room upstairs which
boasted a few chairs, a table and on one wall a wedding
picture of the owner and his bride who lived in the other
half of the house as caretakers. But despite the heat, stink,
and hygienic difficulties, Elsie was clinging courageously to
her doctor husband; maybe the wives had it harder than the
men with more demanding jobs to keep their minds occupied.

"Things move so slowly here," Elsie murmured, looking
sicker every minute. "But Tommy has been given the go-

ahead so we can put in a closed well ourselves—pipe in pure water."

We drove on down the road to the center of the village to inspect the former barracks that might be used as a temporary hospital. It was a big dark barn of a place where squatters were still asleep on eight Army cots because no one had yet kicked them out. Several women, children, and old men opened their eyes, saw we weren't disturbing them, and went back to sleep. Owning nothing at all, they had learned to live in the moment's comfort. But out on the veranda, a young official in a clean white suit rushed, beaming, up to Dr. Whitehall, grasped his hand.

"Doctor, Doctor, you have come!" he cried happily. "You have come at last to take care of my people. They need you so much!"

"Not yet to stay," the doctor said gently. "But soon, I hope."

As we drove away from the disappointed Cai Be official, the doctor sighed, explained this grimy ark could be used temporarily if the really sick patients could be sent to the provincial hospital which was itself understaffed and ill-equipped. What he needed most was a mobile clinic in which he could take modern medicine directly to the people; but no one had yet given the $30,000 to buy and equip such a vehicle. How could you be sure of delivery anyway? This morning when Tommy had gone down to the wharf to collect the three motorcycles needed so badly by the Cai Be staff to get back and forth on the narrow road, he had found that two of the motorcycles already paid for had been stolen and only the chassis of the third was left. So long as "pilferage" was winked at, helping refugees was, indeed, a slow, exasperating business.

The black-market stalls that lined the hot road on our way back nearer to Saigon had become familiar on TV programs. As we slowed for the bottleneck of a patched-up river bridge, we bought hunks of ripe watermelon to soothe our parched throats, stared at tables piled high with Army battle dress, radios, fans, a regular PX. Maybe all this couldn't be stopped. But why couldn't we Americans, if the South Vietnamese could not, protect not only ammunition for guns but at least food and medicines for the refugees, vital ammunition for that psychological war we were always talking about? Was a democracy that ignored thievery from the poor and sick worth dying for?

Asian Christian Relief, however, in spite of all the setbacks, has been able to accomplish a great deal. By common consent, no relief agency in Vietnam works alone but a voluntary council meets to allocate jobs considered most needed by the officials of USAID and of the South Vietnamese government. All the churches, regardless of creeds, whether Quakers, other Protestant denominations, or Roman Catholics work closely with the government agencies, with concerned volunteer Army doctors, with many other private relief groups, none of which are sufficient to meet the swelling need of approximately two million people, rootless, hungry and despairing.

During the first eight months of 1965, when U Thaung Tin opened his Saigon office, the most needed gifts distributed were seven hundred pairs of crutches, given to wounded civilians, many of whom had lost legs in mine explosions.

"I went to the hospital to see one little boy seven years old who'd had both legs blown off," related a member of the Asian staff. "He'd been promised he would walk again on artificial legs. His eyes were like stars when they were strapped on his stumps. He started out eagerly, but, of course, with no preliminary preparation, he fell. He hadn't shed a tear in the hospital up to then though he had lost both his parents and his home, because of his dream of walking again, but as he fell that day, he gave a terrible cry. It was to me the voice of all suffering Vietnam. The nurses rushed to him, got him up on the crutches we had brought.

Now he gets around quite well. He'll learn to use his new legs because he's got back *his hope.*"

Early in 1966, Asian Christian Relief was asked to provide two teams, each with six specialists in medicine, social welfare, nursing, teaching, farming, and construction. They drew their support from churches in Hong Kong, Indonesia, Japan, Korea, Malaysia, Taiwan, Thailand, Australia, New Zealand, with further help from Church World Service in Europe and America and from the Fellowship of the Least Coin. However, their personnel were entirely Asian, eight Australians, two New Zealanders, two Burmese, one from India. The first team under Bruce Hanson of Sydney flew to Tuy Hoa on the sea shore two hundred miles northeast of Saigon, "one of the worst refugee camps in the world."

"Its three thousand refugees live on the shore in rusty tin huts with leaky roofs and the sand for a floor. They have no latrines. Their only water comes from two shallow open wells," wrote a horrified early observer who visited Tuy Hoa in an USAID plane, the only way of access available. "These thousands of refugees, mainly girls, women and children, are facing starvation."

Into this emergency flew Bruce Hanson with five nurses, a social worker, a teacher and a helper in emergency building construction. AID gave the team the use of a house in the village five miles from the camp to live in, but there were no screens (sand fleas can spread malaria, cholera, other diseases), the roof leaked, beds were Army cots, and toilet facilities were crude. The ancient second-hand Land Rover the workers bought in the town nearly collapsed under the load of instruments for the clinic, medicines, and other equipment which had to be transported to and from camp four times a day or every swab and pill would have been stolen. When one is desperate enough whether in New York City or in Tuy Hoa nothing is safe, even when nailed down.

Health conditions in the camp were very bad, as everyone simply used the sand for a bathroom; when a concrete latrine was hastily built, the refugees had no idea what it was for, filled it with rice and other foods to protect them from the rats. "A line of fifteen steel-drum toilets were built, reluctantly viewed at first as an unknown innovation," reads the report of those first days. "Team members coaxed adults [to use them], chased and scolded children found in the wrong places, and brought them back to the latrines, though we still had to clean around them every day. It was at least encouraging that a few of the camp inhabitants gave unsolicited help with the construction work when they saw it going on."

Since no survey had ever been made of the camp's composition or needs, the social worker from India (with the help of six students) registered the refugees as to age, sex, health, means of support. The first figures showed 2,367 persons in 438 families with 1,028 adults and 1,339 children. Half of the families were supported by the fathers who worked at building a new airfield which would soon be finished, throwing them back into unemployment, into the uneasy mob of the untrained laborers in the camp. The farmers could scarcely plant rice in dry sand. The relief workers had hardly finished their survey before it was upset by the arrival of 700 new frightened refugees who had to be housed chiefly in big tents divided by the hung-up clothes they had lugged from the smoking embers of their homes; other arrivals were protected by simply extending from a crowded tent an awning out over the sandy shore. Bruce and his helpers instead of constructing the new school they had planned, had to help devise such hasty shelter for the newcomers.

This influx made even more difficult the work of the new clinic which two nurses held every morning and afternoon, but they managed to treat 1,400 patients the first month, once 147 in a day. Other Asian relief nurses visited in the so-called homes, tents or rusting huts, to treat infections of eye and ear, skin diseases, coughs and other ills simply labeled "fevers" for want of better diagnostic facilities. With the voluntary help of doctors off duty from the nearby military camps, the workers were later able to diagnose malaria in advanced stages which frequently resulted in death, nephritis, tuberculosis, pneumonia, meningitis, cholera and bubonic plague; such very ill patients were transferred to the provincial hospitals for treatment.

Of the 1,300 refugee children, 800 were old enough to go to school but room for only 184 could be found in the local schools at Tuy Hoa, which were five miles away from the camp. The rest, half-sick, hungry and bored, were at a loose end with absolutely nothing to do. The Fellowship of the Least Coin jumped into this dismal picture by providing cash to start a day nursery where the babies of the few fortunate women who could find work in the town could be left in safety and a kindergarten with special furniture for small people, toys, simple playground equipment. If the children could be taught coordination, possibly learn their letters and "numbers," they could go on in school later. Getting materials to the camp by plane for the construction team proved a major problem. The USAID plane did its best, but larger building materials had to be flown in by Army planes, which were usually quite busy transporting military matériel. A great lift for the camp morale were the 1,000 maternity kits distributed by the Asian team to pregnant women, including such necessities as an enamel basin, scissors, needles, thread, bandages, disinfectants and thermometers. Mothers who have their babies in the antiseptic whiteness of the modern hospital delivery room may quail at such a kit but it proved extremely useful when a woman was having a child on the bare floor of a tent where the sand and fleas blew through the unscreened flaps.

U Thaung Tin and his international staff in Saigon have worked day and night to improve conditions. They got hold of a prefabricated building from the government which the construction workers finally found time out from housing

new refugees to erect. The old Land Rover which before
its demise also served to take candidates for baptism to the
sea, and as a transport for the body of a dead Christian
girl to her grave, was replaced by a new vehicle. Also or-
dered were two mobile medical units which it was hoped
wouldn't be stolen from the wharf before delivered; but
these would be a long time arriving as they were too expensive to transport by air to Saigon, as the director of
Asian Relief has been forced to do to safeguard delivery of
smaller items. Some of the one hundred tins of meat shipped
by freighters to be given to blood donors and to refugee
children suffering from malnutrition, as well as tins of milk
for the children's work at Tuy Hoa, were found either too
damaged to use or were stolen as soon as they hit the wharf.
But U Thaung Tin, his smiling, energetic wife, Jim Atkinson, and their staffs go doggedly on, trying to rescue what
they can. Nor is the power of prayer forgotten. There are
regular morning staff team devotions, including Bible reading, hymns, and talks with the Greatest Refugee from the
evil passions of men. Food for the spirit as well as the body
is necessary if one is to go on, day by day, trying to meet
almost overwhelming odds of pilferage, plague, fear, and
lack of hope.

On the credit side of the ledger are the campers who
helped voluntarily in the construction of Tuy Hoa clinic
and school and the two hundred self-help parishioners of the
new Vietnam Evangelical Church at Hoa-Hung, a crowded
suburb of Saigon. There are, of course, many Vietnamese
Buddhists and Roman Catholics but comparatively few Protestants. In 1964 the Fellowship of the Least Coin gave a
small group of these Saigonese a lift by helping them build
their church after the banks had given them all the loan possible. Now the Hoa-Hung church has a mixed congregation
of ninety families, many unemployed, some paratroopers
from the barracks across the busy street that runs to the
airport. The group also included masons, university stu-

dents, and businessmen who have managed by building with their own hands and by sacrificial giving to complete the small white church with its Cross and open Bible over the door. They have almost paid off the bank loan! Besides the weekday Bible classes, the building is used every Sunday for an early morning prayer meeting, then for Sunday School, adult morning service, young people's Bible class, and evening prayer. Now the energetic members feel that the time has come to have a daily school built upon the roof and maybe to open another small Evangelical church down the street.

Far different from the tiny Protestant Chapel was the huge Buddhist temple, the Xa Loi Pagoda with its great Buddha, its political power, and its block-long school protected by barbed wire. When I went inside and stood looking up at the bronze Buddha who dominates the temple, a priest in an orange robe sidled up to me to ask, "Wouldn't you like to see the martyrs? They're back here, in the room behind the Buddha."

"The ones who burned themselves up with kerosene? No, thank you."

"Is only pictures," he assured me. "Come."

The photographs were very poor; the priest remarked cheerfully that burning one's body was just like taking off an old dress and putting on a new one. "The spirit is the real person and it does not change or hurt," he insisted. "One gains great credit by burning." He looked pointedly at the poor box so I put in a coin and held out to him an address in Vietnamese. The clerk at the American Embassy had told me that at the Chaplain General's office I could find out the whereabouts of a boy from my own home town whom I wanted to invite to dinner if he was within asking distance. The priest assured me, "Is very near here. I tell the taxi driver the address for you."

The taxis are very small, dart ahead at neck-jerking speed, and the drivers know little if any English, but I watched the street signs and numbers till finally I saw the building I wanted. It was a large white former villa with a single sentry out in front, holding a rifle and looking very hot in his uniform. "Stop!" I told my taxi driver. "This is where I want to get out! Please, stop!" Instead, he gave one frightened look, put his foot on the accelerator. He knew the address already, yet the louder I demanded to get out, the faster he went, till, exasperated, I finally opened the car door and he drew up reluctantly to the curb. Very angry, I tossed him what I owed; now I would have to walk back six blocks with the thermometer over one hundred. I was still fuming when I arrived at the American sentry. He pushed back his helmet, explained in his soft Alabama voice, "Ma'am, if that taxi man had stopped in front of a guarded military installation, I'd'a had to shoot him, daid."

We were back in Saigon, churches or no churches, and there was "a war on, lady." Only last week an officers' billet a couple of blocks from my hotel had been bombed and several Americans killed. The constant shadow of death was hard to believe in when you've just had tea and cakes at a friendly little Protestant Church, and then talked with an orange-robed priest who served the gentle Gautama Buddha who had advised, "a clansman [should] minister to his friends and familiars . . . by treating them as he treats himself."

I went back to my hotel, "beat up" in mind and body, limp and discouraged. This war was such a mixed-up mess. Could a handful of Asian church relief workers, even if they did understand the Vietnamese way of thinking, really accomplish anything? It seemed rather like putting a Band-Aid upon a gaping wound. The bare-faced arrogance of that black market stuff selling so openly! Was it worth what we were paying not only in money but in people killed in battle, kidnaped and then shot, to make a few black market millionaires, whether they were Vietnamese, American, or European? There wasn't enough cash in the world to pay for the life of one boy if he happened to belong to you. Off the record, how did our G.I.'s feel about all this?

In this mood, I happened to discover a little sidewalk café where Americans and Vietnamese were sitting at long tables, sipping tall cool drinks and watching the red-hot traffic roll by; everyone was talking with everyone else as you do at a fire or a war. Queer how secret thoughts you wouldn't admit to a friend pour out to an anonymous stranger whom you'll never see again. To the G.I.s lounging at my table I was from home and that was sufficient introduction even for a lady long past the whistle stage. Since Saigon is off limits for many, most of the military were waiting for planes to carry them either for R and R—Rest and Recreation—or were on their way back home, to Colorado, California, Pennsylvania, and Oregon. One boy wore a Montagnard brass bracelet made from shell casing which meant he'd been adopted by the mountain people—a Special Forces soldier, Green Beret. Two others were from an American tank corps. Two who had been fighting up by the DMZ were en route for two weeks in Hawaii. This was a mixed group whose opinions might not be definitive but who had seen death intimately in jungles, rice fields, mountains, and villages. After all, how these G.I.s felt about this war they were slogging out might well be the determining factor in defeat or victory. Anyone could pull the trigger of a gun; it was the spirit behind this which counted. What did they feel about the suddenly converted conscientious objectors at home who were valiantly burning their draft cards?

"Those longhairs don't bother me because they don't know what they're talking about," said the Special Forces boy impatiently. "It's like Calvin Coolidge saying he was against sin—we all are against war. Especially we who are fighting it. But if we let down South Vietnam and Thailand when we've promised to help them, we'd have to fight this out eventually either in China, or perhaps at home. When a burglar's at your door, you don't just say, 'Welcome!' "

The Green Beret boy had had two years at college in Oregon before he joined the Army. When he saw me trying not to look at the scars on his face and neck from leeches, bad diet, and jungle rot, he explained that he'd been a year and a half up near the border of Laos, one of two American advisors to a battalion of South Vietnamese. This outfit had also included Montagnards and some Chinese who had fled from Communist China. Because the whirlybirds came in to camp only twice a week with ammunition and food, then took back a load of refugees, the American boys had had to get along mostly on local food. "Fortunately, I like rice." He grinned. "And we had good fruit. Every now and then the Montagnards had a feast, killed a cow, and when I drank the blood with them, they took me into the gang." He looked down at his shiny brass bracelet proudly. "Usually you could trust them best of any of the Vietnamese we were 'advising.' " His face hardened. "There's always been graft but when it gets up to the brass . . . we found out that the commanding officer, the South Vietnamese in charge of the camp, was charging the refugees from the devastated villages for the trip back in American helicopters! Only those got chosen who had the right price!"

His hand tightened on his cold glass, loosened deliberately as he admitted, "I suppose goofs like that happen in any army. After all, it's made up of all kinds. But the villagers and the mountain people I liked a lot. I'm going back home now to finish college but I learned more here than in any university classroom. I learned what kind of pay really satisfies your guts. When the war's over, I'd like to come back to these village people. They need practically everything and the more I learn, the more I can offer them. I'm sure going home with a different attitude; the rest of the world isn't just a many-colored map: it's people." He admitted wryly, "Maybe I just grew up."

"It ain't so bad here if you're not snagged by a sniper or

don't step on a mine," agreed another boy in uniform. "The real enemies are not the jungle Charlies but the inside thugs. The wrong people making money outa the wrong things, sickness, burnt houses 'n legless kids."

"But what can we do about it?" demanded another G.I. hotly. "If we really took over, we'd be called the 'Great American Dictators.' "

"They call us that anyway," retorted another boy in uniform. "So what difference does that make? What does it matter if *we* know we're *not?* I believe in *doing* something about what we say we believe." He added apologetically to me, "That'd cost a lot more taxes for you at home, I reckon."

"This is our war, too," I reminded him. "We should help pay for it. Everyone fights in his own way."

I told them about meeting that morning the two girl nurses on a relief team who'd lain for two nights of terror under their Army cots while the VC and South Vietnamese had carefully shot around the village house where they had their clinic because both sides needed the medical care it represented. The shaken girls, allowed to leave when the battle was over, had come down to Saigon "for a rest" which heaven knew their shattered nerves needed, but they were going back tomorrow. Then there were the 1,300 children at Tuy Hoa where the Fellowship of the Least Coin were helping, and the Asian Church Service doctor who was taking his young wife with him to live in Cai Be, trying to make a small dent in a vast medical problem. "The little people in these villages just want peace," murmured the Oregon boy who was going home to college so he could come back here to help them.

"Who doesn't?" The tall pale G.I. sitting at the end of our table hadn't said a word before, just sat there, stirring the ice in his tall glass with his finger. "There was a loot in the hospital at Denang, a nurse. She stuck a thermometer in my face so I couldn't talk back, and starts dreaming. "Tomorrow I go R and R to Singapore! I gotta real cool hotel, the red-

velvet Raffles, no less. I'll get a manicure, a facial, the works
—and buy me a new dress to wear to dinner. But first, I'm
gonna take *two* baths, one to soak clean and the other to
wash this place right out'a my hair—for ten whole days!' "

They don't have to like it, but they're doing their jobs,
these boys and girls of ours. No, men and women. When I
met him on the sidewalk at Saigon, one stranger G.I. offered eagerly to carry my heavy bag so he could talk with me
about a little town in Texas. These young Americans were a
more tolerant generation than mine had been. Who was it
that had mourned that there was a "moral vacuum among
the young in the United States"? I was glad I had not presented my letters of introduction to the ambassador or to
the high government officials in Saigon; that I had listened
instead to these citizens, some of whom were too young to
vote, speaking their free democratic minds. "A most remarkable generation," Senator J. W. Fulbright has called them,
"who are striving to keep alive the traditional values of
American democracy." *

Back in Boston, however, when I met by accident a high-
ranking member of the Diplomatic Corps, I was curious to
know what he would make of the G.I. bull session. As a
Vietnam tourist, I admitted that I knew no definitive answers, that my account was valuable only as it told the folks
back home who wanted to know what was happening not
only to the bodies of their men but in their minds. I asked
the official, did the government really think we could win
this war both coming and going, so to speak, with a gun or
a napalm bomb in one hand and a bag of fertilizer or a school
book in the other?

This man who had spent twenty years in trouble spots in
the Far East hesitated, replied at first with stock answers that
if we didn't prop up Vietnam as promised, the surrounding
countries would surely collapse to the Reds; that it was im-

* Senator J. W. Fulbright, "The Great Society Is A Sick Society," *The New
York Times Magazine,* August 20, 1967.

possible to eradicate "squeeze" in business in the East; that there simply weren't enough men or money available to stop theft. The experiment in the power of prayer by the Fellowship of the Least Coin was rather idealistic, wasn't it?

"Yes," I agreed. "You think I shouldn't wave the flag about what a Christian democracy *means?* About the kids and their thinking straight?"

He said, "I'll never forgive you if you don't."

Eight

Pioneer in the Philippines

A SLUM IS BASICALLY a state of mind, a resentment that the good things which make life worthwhile have passed you by and that no one cares, that the more you try to climb out of the muddy morass of poverty, ignorance and fear, the deeper you sink back—so what's the use of trying? This psychosomatic sickness of apathy, loss of ambition which eats into a man's spirit as cancer may into his body, can attack whether its victims live in the concrete streets of a great city where the fire and ambulance sirens scream or among lovely, lonely green hills where the tall trees whisper, birds sing, and flowers flame. But sometimes a very small dose of hope or the ointment of self-respect can cure this "slum sickness."

Such was the experience of the Bila-an farmers, aborigines who live in the almost inaccessible hill country of Mindanao in the Philippines. They raised small crops of corn and copra, but to get these to market was a nearly insurmountable problem. Since there were no proper roads in the hills, the farmers and their families had to carry the heavy bags of corn on their heads down the steep, slippery paths or pole the produce down mountain streams on precarious rafts. Pack horses could carry heavy loads but a horse cost more cash than the average man could save in many years and the national highway to the city, when reached, was long, hot, and dangerous with many sly thieves.

153

Usually the farmer sold to any passing trucker who might or might not shortchange him. Or possibly the market would be glutted with corn at this moment. In any case, the money from his crop seldom paid for enough seed to plant again, for the rags of cloth to cover the nakedness of his family.

The Sarangani Farmers Cooperative, where the hill farmers could combine their small crops into larger more profitable loads, was made possible by the gift of a three-quarter-ton truck, a former weapons carrier, by the Fellowship of the Least Coin to collect the produce and carry it directly to the city for sale.

"The Pioneer, as we named the gift truck, was a small key to a very big closed door," related one church worker who with his wife had lived for ten years among the Bila-an aborigines. "This World War II surplus vehicle could carry thirty bags of shelled corn, nearly a ton, to the market. It proved to be very adaptable to the kind of terrain in our area, hilly, with no decent roads, and very muddy during the rainy months from October to February. By following the valley paths in the wet season and in the dry months, the river beds, the Pioneer could make the trip. Farmers would be notified when to bring down their two or three bags and had only to carry the crop a short way over the steep hills to be picked up. We even built a bodega [warehouse] where the cooperative crops could be stored till the market price made it advantageous to sell."

At first the commercial truckers who had been able to pick up the crops at their own price on the national highway were understandably angry and stirred up the local community to stymie this cooperative effort.

"All kinds of sabotage were resorted to," relates an early member ruefully. "Nails in the mud to ruin the Pioneer's tires, trails mysteriously blocked with fallen trees and rocks. But gradually it became evident that getting better prices for the farmers' crops was helping the whole area. The coop farmers, encouraged by better, more assured sales, were clearing more of their land. With a spark of hope that, after all, they might make a decent living they opened up untouched portions, planted more varied marketable crops. The commercial truckers were forced to raise their own prices and the community came to see that the Pioneer meant more cash for everyone. So the sabotage stopped."

"The Pioneer also saved lives," reports Reverend Lorenzo Genotiva, who helped organize the cooperative and lived through the first exciting days of the venture. "When a woman was dying because of hemorrhage which no one was able to stop, no other vehicle would take her into town for fear she would die, en route, and a corpse is considered very bad luck. The Pioneer carried the very sick patient to the doctor just in time to save her life."

He added thoughtfully, "The women of Asia gave us their Least Coins, perhaps an insignificant amount, to buy a second-hand truck. A few drops of water are not much, but to a desert-thirsty man they may mean his very life.

"But more important than the trucking job the Pioneer did was the understanding that came to us in our forgotten corner of the world, just beginning to clamor for the comforts of life which other people had been long enjoying, that we had friends. There were actually sisters in Christ whom we would probably never see who cared enough to help us live better. We were aware that these women who gave were not those of great means but out of the abundance of their hearts, they gave. . . . It encouraged our own people to bestir themselves. Sitio people widened their trails, excavated hillsides, straightened sharp curves so that the Pioneer could pass."

Thus a truck which formerly carried weapons of war now brought back from the city coconut seedlings for the farmers to plant between their rows of corn. Ammunition of good will.

It was especially appropriate that the Fellowship of the Least Coin should offer help here in the Philippines, where

Shanti Solomon had first conceived the idea of small giving and large prayers while she was waiting in Manila for the rest of the international Fellowship team to get back from Korea, where she, as an Indian, had been refused admittance. Felicidad Catli, a leader among Christian church women as well as principal of the Ellinwood Teachers College, took me to the Ellinwood Malate church center, where Shanti had met with the group of Filipino women who were "searching the Bible for wisdom to forgive our former enemies."

"After our suffering during the Japanese occupation, when we lost husbands, sons and watched friends die of hunger in the prison camp, when our homes had been shelled and flattened, we had much to forgive. Our Bible study group was a mixed one including women from all walks of life, a bishop's wife, a public school teacher, wives of bankers and businessmen who were trying to patch up their affairs after the ravages of war, a lady lawyer, a trained woman pharmacist, a supervisor of several private schools; most of us were also housewives. We were glad to have Shanti join us, but we were startled when she cried out as we were reading about the widow's mite, 'That's it! We can prove our reconciliation by praying for each other around the world . . . and by giving the least coins of our country to anyone who needs them. Alone, the coin may be almost worthless but if you give yourself, the gift is big!' "

Felicidad smiled, remembering how eagerly these Filipino women from all walks of life had carried the vision of the international prayer fellowship back to their many congregations. As the first president of the women's organization of the Church of Christ in the Philippines, an amalgamation of many Protestant denominations, Felicidad herself "was able to bring the Fellowship to a national level."

"We saved our Least Coins at first in coconut shells, in bamboo sticks, in discarded sugar bags, anything handy, since when giving only one centavo a month [a fourth of an American penny] we could easily spend more to buy the containers than we gave. Even so, in many of the smaller churches, hard hit by the war, the women did not even have that tiny coin to spare. One asked me anxiously, 'Will it be all right if I give an egg instead? Or a handful of rice when the crop comes in?'

" 'An egg is worth four American pennies; it will do for the year,' I told her firmly for she must understand that the money was not the main gift. 'But you can pray every month with love for a Japanese, a German or perhaps for a Korean or an American woman.' "

There is an old saying in the Philippines, "The man is the head of the house but the woman is the treasurer, so that men's trousers do not need pockets!" Felicidad urged her Protestant women, many of whom could not read, to join in Roman Catholic prayer customs. The country is over ninety percent of this faith, a heritage from the early Spanish fathers. "When the Angelus rings at six, drop your work, also, stop wherever you are, in the kitchen, in the fields, in a jitney and remember another woman just like you in Thailand, India, Yugoslavia. Say a word of prayer that we may all be sisters. Every Christian can listen for the Angelus and remember."

Felicidad was not surprised when several Roman Catholic women asked if they might join the Fellowship "as individual givers" as did "some Moslem women of a large mind. Once a year all women are invited to take part in the dedication of the small coins, which usually takes place during one of the yearly Church of Christ conferences. Then the women bring their collected centavos, their eggs or bananas, lay them upon the altar. We use for this service the Book of Prayer collected and published by the church women of Hong Kong."

"I have been privileged to go to the United States, to Europe, to see much of Asia, but even illiterate rural women can become world conscious," Felicidad explains. "Wherever

I go, I take my projector, show my women slides of how people eat and live in other countries. When I showed Filipino housewives the mothers in Japan preparing a meal, farm women whispered, excited, 'Why, they eat rice as we do!' "

So many Filipino women have joined the Fellowship of the Least Coin that today they are furnished with an inexpensive envelope in which to save their centavos, on the back of which is printed: *"Monthly prayer concern around the world:* January, Thailand; Switzerland; February, Ceylon, Burma . . ."* and so on through the rest of the year. The giver is urged, "Place on the blank space the *date* of the month you have designated for a definite prayer day." "Thus," Felicidad explains, "we go together to the Source of all inner strength."

Felicidad is another of the highly educated, much-traveled women who are channels of international understanding. Born in Luzon, she first went to school in her home town, then took her bachelor of theology degree at the Union Theological Seminary in Manila. When her husband, Rev. Samuel Catli, was sent to the Yale School of Divinity for further study, Felicidad went too, was awarded her master's in Religious Education. "Our scholarships there were part of the rehabilitation after the war," she explains. The Catlis, now back in Manila, have three children, scattered about the globe; one son is an architect; another daughter is doing graduate work in nutrition at Michigan State in East Lansing; while the baby, Felicidad Junior, is just entering college as a freshman student of the arts in her home city. For such families there is, indeed, "no East nor West."

Samuel Catli, now director of Christian Education and Literature for the National Council of Churches in Manila is a thin, smiling man who prepared for the first Asian Youth Assembly, held at Silliman University in 1965, "A Brief History of the Philippines" ranging from 1542, when the islands were named in honor of Prince Filipe, son of Charles the First and heir to the Spanish throne, to July 4, 1946, when the flag of the new Republic flew alone for the first time, a flag long-loved, "red, white, and blue with a sun and three stars, as consecrated and honored by the people and recognized by law." His pride gleamed through his passionate words to the young leaders of other developing countries:

The three five-pointed stars represent the three geographical divisions of the Philippines namely Luzon, Visayas, and Mindanao. The sun represents the light of freedom and justice, while the equilateral triangle means equality under the law. The blue field is a symbol of loyalty, patriotism and honor, while the red stands for valor and self-sacrifice.

The flag unfurled on June 12, 1898, was made in Hong Kong by Mrs. Marcela de Agoncillo, who shared the patriotic fervor of the revolutionaries.

For some time during the early part of the American occupation, the Philippine flag was not allowed to be flown, but later its use was permitted along with the United States flag. It was replaced during the early part of World War II by the Japanese flag. It was a proud day in the life of the nation when the Stars and Stripes of the United States was hauled down on July 4, 1946, to make way for the Tri-color of the Philippines to wave all alone over a free and independent nation.

This Filipino family illustrates a love of one's own country which does not preclude but rather enhances understanding of patriots in other nations, just as people of differing faiths may enjoy a rich diversity and at the same time cooperate in helping the needy of the world.

This 1965 Asian Youth Assembly at Dumaguete seemed worthy of support to the Fellowship of the Least Coin, since it was "the first time . . . five hundred young men and women from fifteen Asian countries had come together to live, study, and discuss and learn more about each other's

ways of . . . thinking." One young delegate wrote back, "It
was indeed an ecumenical assembly, for in the opening service
and in the panel discussion a Roman Catholic Bishop and a
priest welcomed all the delegates and participated in the
discussion.

"During the weekend all the delegates were sent to live
with the Filipino folks in different homes and towns. Some
hostesses were Roman Catholic, some were Independent
Church members, and some were other Protestants.

"The climax of the Assembly was when we had Holy
Communion together in the Church despite all the differences in practices. We bore in mind our oneness in Christ as
we sang together, 'One Lord, one faith, one birth . . .' "

The root of the problem of aborigines adjusting to the
modern world, however, lay deeper than helping mountain
farmers to market corn and copra. The Bila-ans were only
one tribe of "neglected cultural minorities." The National
Commission on Integration set up by the Philippine government discovered that eighty percent of these primitive people, 1,700,000 citizens, neglected because they were apart
in remote regions, lived on the island of Mindanao.

"Many of these people were Moslems, others were animists.
These latter were of great interest to anthropologists, but
the church's mission was to regard them not as curiosities
which so-called civilization had left behind but as *people*
whose culture we must respect. At the same time we must
lead them out of a religion of fear to a God of mercy,"
Dr. Alexander Grant, the acting director of the Christian
Institute for Study of Ethnic Communities in Asia, explained. He had recently returned to Manila from a post-
graduate seminar at Cornell University. "They needed to
know that they were not merely trembling victims to be
punished at the whim of an angry spirit." In order to treat
these cultural minorities intelligently, it was necessary to
understand their way of life. Native leaders who had been
educated in Christian schools, many of them college gradu-

ates, were selected to study further the backgrounds of their own people. The Christian Institute for the Study of Ethnic Communities was set up in Manila originally with a small grant from the Fellowship of the Least Coin, but other groups soon joined in the research project.

"These animists have been labeled 'pagan' but if you define 'pagan' as 'irreligious,' this is not strictly true," explained Dr. Grant. "The spirit world is an integral part of their daily lives. The first thing a housewife does when she prepares the main meal of the day is to put a handful of rice aside for the spirits. The hunter prays before he sets out into the forest to shoot deer or pigs and when he is successful, he offers thanks with food for the spirits before he or his people eat the meat. There are numerous offerings also on special occasions such as weddings, harvests, funerals. Religion to the animist is not a thing set apart but important in everything he does. But he gives more through fear than love.

"In the remote districts of the Philippines, the aborigines had clung more rigidly to the idea of the perpetuation of family or tribe, and it was important not to take away the rules governing daily living from these people without giving them something better. Anything else means chaos as has been proven in Africa, many other similar situations. The modern Christian missionary dares to be exposed to ideas other than his own, to first understand, then adapt to the good in cultural values. He uses this reverence for spiritual matters positively to explain that Jesus Christ is a spirit who brought love into the world, that fear and hatred died upon the Cross, not just a man's body."

The Institute, which was designed to study the mores of not only neglected minorities in the Philippines, but also those in Ceylon, Pakistan, India, Burma, Thailand, Taiwan, Malaya, Indonesia, Papua, and New Guinea, began in a modest way in three large rooms in a new building lent them by St. Andrews' Episcopal Theological Seminary in

Manila. A graduate student at the University of the Philippines, Rufino Tima, did research "concerning health and healing under the impact of modern medicine among the Colingas in the northern Philippines."

"Modern medical science has made great advances, but it can still learn something about psychosomatic healing from these primitive people," Dr. Grant insists. "True they know nothing of the germ theory and attribute disease chiefly to having angered a spirit. However, not only the patient but the whole community believe implicitly in the power of the *walian,* the witch doctor. The sick man who *believes* implicitly that he will get well, who is the center of community attention, often does recover. This does not mean advocating the scrapping of modern medicine; far from it. But if you add such mental attitudes to modern drugs and treatments, you get results, not only among aborigines!

"We have modern demons, too, not only in rain forests but in our so-called civilized democracies," Dr. Grant points out vigorously. "Demons of violence, of blatant nationalism. All over the world the American spirit is being equated with material success, powerful guns, the Bomb. The real genius of America is quite different. The power behind the Pilgrims who struggled against sickness, death, and the harshness of nature in the New World, was a firm belief in a personal God and man's right to choose his own way to worship him."

Under the aegis of the new Institute, a graduate student in Manila, Rev. P. Moasosang, began a study of his own people back home in Assam, India. His study of "The Effect of the Christian Mission upon the Social and Religious Organization of the AO Nagas" was so unique and definitive that when it was submitted to the Hartford Theological Seminary in the United States, they granted him his Master of Arts degree as a result of his research. When Moasosang went back to Calcutta to give a paper upon "The Naga Search for Self-identify" at a consultation between the leaders of Nagaland and the Indian Central Government, they were so impressed that he was invited to become principal of the Baptist English School at Kohima, Assam. In this Indian school of high standing among whose seven hundred students all Naga tribes are represented, this young man, deeply grateful for what the Fellowship of the Least Coin has done to assist him, will be able to put into practice some of the ideas which he explored at the Institute in Manila.

"This is merely a small beginning," he explains. "Taiwan has also been here studying what we are researching and how they may adapt our findings to work among their own mountain people." Thus science, native culture and the Christian religion combine to lead forgotten aborigines, in terms they can understand, into a brighter day. It is heartening that the prayers of women all over the world have helped spark these scientific "beginnings." Mr. Moasosang remarks that the Institute is "a significant pioneering venture of the churches of Asia to better understand their mission in Asia."

The trek of thousands of these untrained tribal people into the city in search of education and a better income has almost overwhelmed the city of Manila with squatters, as well as taxing the welfare and health facilities of the new Republic. In 1946 Manila had only 23,000 of these unskilled migrants, but by 1965 the invasion had grown to 282,730 squatters. Since these homeless immigrants had no money to pay for accommodations, they built makeshift huts from any materials they could find or steal upon government-owned park land or in any empty vacant lot, no matter to whom it might belong. They had no toilet facilities, no idea of modern hygiene, so that disease soon became rampant. Public agencies were overwhelmed. Unskilled jobs were very hard to find; 80 percent of those who lived crowded into Manila slum apartments had only part-time jobs; even factories required a high school education for their workers. Crime, adolescent violence, thieving, and habitual idle drunkenness grew into such desperate problems that the Philippine government had to do something drastic to try to solve them.

The new settlement at Sepang Palay was at least a partial answer. Twenty-three thousand squatters were picked up by government trucks and transported forty kilometers into the hills north of Manila and given land. They were furnished materials with which to build their own houses, and many did an excellent job of making neat homes with verandas looking out over the brown rolling hills, with well-kept yards, gardens, even outhouses. Others still kept to their primitive hygiene, but as one worker commented, "At least here there is sun and air to fumigate!" The big problem was water. The countryside is very dry and while many government wells were dug, they proved far from enough for the community. The public faucets might be a mile or so away from the house so that it took several members of the family all day simply to stand in the long lines to get sufficient water to drink and bathe, let alone to nourish the vegetable gardens where they were supposed to grow their own food.

The women and children in the Sepang Palay settlement became the concern of the Fellowship of the Least Coin as well as of many other church and philanthropic people. Mrs. Fannie So, a Chinese banker's wife who has eight children of her own but who gives every Saturday, helping as a nurse in the free clinic of the Interchurch Community Center, drove Felicidad Catli, another Fellowship member, and me out to Sepang Palay to lunch with the pastor and his wife who were in charge. The day was unbearably hot and the road rough, unpaved, so that as traffic passed us, the perspiration running down your face and the back of your legs turned to mud, for it was impossible to keep the car windows closed. The women and children we passed trudging through the dust on the endless pilgrimage for water looked as uncomfortable as we were. The only ones who smiled at us were the naked brown children wearing only cocked hats of newspaper upon their heads against the blistering sun. It was a relief to arrive at the Interchurch Center in Area B, where a Filipino pastor cried, "Mabuhay—welcome!" and his hospitable wife offered us cool drinks of orange soda water.

There are approximately one thousand families in Area B. Only twenty-two teachers for this district of Sepang Palay have been sent out by the government, and there are as yet so few schoolhouses that many classes have to meet in the local homes. The day nursery and kindergarten whose teacher is supported by the Fellowship of the Least Coin have one hundred and sixty pupils, aged three to seven years, who meet, half in the morning and half in the afternoon, in a long shedlike room where the small tables and chairs for the children are roughly home-made. The toys are bottle tops, games of sticks which the children have collected themselves; to youngsters who have nothing, self-help and ingenuity are important lessons. The pupils are taught by the student intern native dancing, music, and finger painting for coordination, as well as personal hygiene.

"The girl student has to love people and have real concern to work here during her junior year; then she goes back to finish her senior year at college," Felicidad explained. As director for the Ellinwood College of Christian Education, which includes training for preschool, elementary, and secondary teachers, she oversees the program for these youngsters from the squatter families. The young intern reported, "Last week we 'graduated' seventy of the nursery school babies into kindergarten with proper ceremonies, which, of course, meant a party! The chief thing the children come for is to be fed; for many, the porridge of cornmeal or wheat mixed with rolled oats, sugar, and milk is the only meal they get for the day."

"If the camote crop is good, we give each child one also," interposed the pastor, in whose dark face bright gold teeth gleamed. The Young Dentists Association offer a clinic here three times a week with a charge of only fifty centavos. In addition, volunteer Manila doctors whom Mrs. So assists run the free weekly clinic.

"The camote is a kind of sweet potato, especially suited

to this dry soil, which in such a climate takes only three months to mature," the pastor explained. They looked appetizing on the luncheon table as we sat down; the young intern was trying valiantly to brush off the flies as there were no funds available to buy screens for the windows or doors. Felicidad had wrapped some sandwiches for me in waxed paper, explaining ruefully that my not accepting the pastor's wife's hospitality was not due to bad manners but to a "bug" I had picked up in Singapore. The pastor, eating heartily, went on to tell us how every bit of the camote was useful. The leaves made excellent salad (vitamin C), the stalk could be "slipped" for planting in the squatters' gardens, the roots had plenty of protein, and any stalks that were left could be fed to the pigs. Or if the neighborhood farmers had any extra camotes, they could be sold to dealers coming out from Manila; here at Sepang Palay the farmers received only two pesos (twenty-five cents) for a five-gallon can of camotes which could be sold in Manila for six. Besides demonstrating the uses of the camote, the pastor also supervised the pigs sent from the United States by the Heifer Program which distributes animals to farmers in many lands, as gifts from American farmers. Would I like to see his prize porkers? They looked camote-plump and their pens were neater than some of the squatters' front yards. The boar was loaned out to the local farmers with the understanding that the first piglet of the litter would be given to another ambitious owner to feed and care for.

"Our work will be easier here if we ever get our own well," the pastor suggested to Felicidad and her friends. Five sections of pipe which had to go down 150 feet to avoid contamination of the water were still needed and "cash to pay for the dig." They promised to look for proper pipes, we thanked the slender hostess exhausted by cooking lunch for so many, and left in our sun-baked car for the air-conditioned hotel back in Manila. These pioneer families desperately needed water, screens, markets for their garden crops, but at least they owned the roofs under which they slept.

"Social conditions are bad in Sepang Palay," admitted Felicidad as we gulped new dust clouds. "Since there are no jobs, factories, or businesses here, most of the men go back to Manila during the week to try to pick up a few pesos. When the bus comes back from the city about seven p.m. every weekend, mothers keep their young girls close at home, for many of the men have earned just enough to buy them a few hours of forgetfulness at the nearest bar. Families here who want to bring up their children as good citizens have a hard time."

"But isn't that a policeman over there?" I queried. "At the side of the road."

"Rural police. They get only their guns and uniforms, no pay. It's a difficult job. In such a mixed group, gathered up, willy-nilly, from the squatter city huts, there are bound to be some bad citizens."

To meet such a herculean problem of settling into these arid hills twenty-three thousand peso-less people, even if they are willing to help themselves, takes all the ingenuity of the government, the churches, both the Protestants and the Roman Catholics who are now in the process of building a large school, and of private agencies and interested good citizens, like Mrs. So, Felicidad, and her sister Christians in the Fellowship of the Least Coin.

As the hot and cold water gushed into my immaculate tub in my tiled bathroom at the Manila Hotel, and the air-conditioning blew gratefully through my wet hair washed in the shower because I couldn't wait for the tub to fill, it didn't seem fair that some of us had been born to such luxury and others to thirst and flies. Would they find enough pipe for the well at Sepang Palay? Maybe the Prithipuri home in Ceylon wasn't so badly off, after all; at least they had a river running close by in which to wash four hundred diapers and eighty-five retarded children.

Nine

Stars in the Dark

> *We have grasped the mystery of the atom and re-*
> *jected the Sermon on the Mount. The world has*
> *achieved brilliance without wisdom, power with-*
> *out conscience. Ours is a world of nuclear giants*
> *and ethical infants. We know more about war*
> *than we know about peace, more about killing*
> *than we know about living.*
>
> GENERAL OMAR BRADLEY

"GIVING IN THE UNITED STATES has become a status symbol," grumbled a businessman recently as he handed over his check for fifty dollars to the United Fund. "If I don't give as much as I did last year, my neighbor who is collecting thinks I'm a cheap skate. So I give a little more to keep up my image. Actually my income tax blank has the last word; to get deductions, I give for projects, churches, schools, strange diseases no one I knew ever had, seldom to individuals just because they need it. Let them apply to welfare or social security. The trouble with a socialized state is that it has a mechanical heart.

"It used to be different when I was a child. I was raised on a small subsistence farm where we never had much cash

169

but we were independent. The worst disgrace that could
happen to anyone was to 'go on the town' for relief. We gave
what we could spare; not a very big sum, I grant you, but we
gave directly to the man who needed it, not to a vague 'cause.'
Spontaneous person-to-person giving is out. We seldom hand
over a few bucks just because a human need touches our
heart. If the gift without the giver is bare, we do not give
at all."

How to make institutionalized giving more human, more
suited to the individual needs of the have-nots, and at the
same time not kill the self-respect and the initiative of the
recipient, is the big problem that worries not only Congress
but the very poor who perforce have to take the hand-outs.
A minimum federally guaranteed income simply compounds
the problem rather than answering it, a device of "ethical
infants," as many welfare recipients know by experience.

"A government subsidy, welfare, or whatever name you
call it, is only a one-way street, you can never go back," one
mother in East Harlem who is trying to raise five children
alone in a housing project explained to me, with tears in
her concerned brown eyes. "I want my kids to be self-re-
specting, *independent* citizens. Welfare shuts you into a
tight shell of being scared, scared if you're taking it you're
ruining the kids' get-up-and-go, scared if you don't, they
won't eat. You don't dare take a chance on getting a job;
you might lose it if you did. So maybe you cheat a little, lie
a little just to keep the cash coming. I ask you, what kind
of a home can be built on lying and cheating? It's just a
cheap boarding house the kids get out of as quick as they
can. With pot, if they can't escape any other way. What we
need is jobs that pay enough to live on, not more hand-outs."

This same twisted psychology that ignores the emotional
reactions of discouraged people applies internationally. Instead of The Ugly Americans we should be labeled The
Childish Americans, who think that by sharing a half-licked
lollypop in our favorite democratic flavor we can make peo-

ple love us. We mismanage our international giving even more naively than our federal or state welfare by disregarding as unimportant the very human humiliation of those who must always receive, never reciprocate. We expect the "developing nations," whatever their native culture, whether like the Masai they prefer a cup of cow's blood and milk to hamburgers and hot dogs, to leap with joy at being invited to become carbon copies of ourselves. Whether it be the Russians trying to sell communism or us peddling a democracy which caters to the color of a man's skin (few Asians or Africans have white skins or want them) the receiving nations accept the massive grants of wheat, guns, or planes with tongue in cheek. Is a quid pro quo a gift or a bribe? Even many church foundations are suspect. As one Israeli mother pointed out wryly, "They don't seem to realize that Jesus was not 'made in-Detroit'; He was a Jew in the Middle East." Should we be surprised when "receiving nations," with a childish irritation equal to our own, vote against us in the United Nations, burn our embassies and libraries?

When the American in Manila had wondered if her country women would be interested in saving "twelve piddling pennies a year," Shanti, the Indian woman, had warned, "If you do not, you Americans will be the loneliest women in the world." Charity turned sour becomes violence, as Detroit, Watts, and many other American cities have found out. *Reciprocal* giving breeds self-respect, spiritual wealth. One businessman put it, "If we are to give any substance to the American dream, we must get back to giving as individuals, not en masse."

This understanding that the *way* in which people give is as important as the cash is the reason that the Fellowship of the Least Coin with very little organization but spread by eager word of mouth, is today giving and receiving in twenty-nine countries on six continents.

One Brazilian woman who was mounting the ramp of a plane in Rio, carrying a paper bag full of centavos to be deposited in her church women's headquarters for Fellowship relief work, was dismayed when the bag broke and the cash scattered all over the asphalt below. "Money, money!" yelled the bystanders, snatching at the coins, but when they looked closer, they threw them back down again, for a handful was almost worthless. Yet the prayers and real concern for the despair of women in other countries pay dividends far beyond the size of the comparatively small cash gifts by the Fellowship of the Least Coin for they aid chiefly *projects already begun by the recipients* who know that some of these coins come from women as poor as they are.

During the twenty-two-day war between Pakistan and India, one Indian woman, dressed in her distinctive sari, was distributing blankets given by the Fellowship of the Least Coin, in the Pakistani refugee camp. She and one of the Pakistani women paused to listen together to a radio broadcast of how the battle was raging between their respective countries. Suddenly the Moslem woman seized the hand of the enemy Christian and cried, "I hope all is well with you and yours."

It is further significant that the Least Coin Fellowship was begun and is carried on by *women*. As one American put it, "We who are the mothers, sisters or wives of scientists, hippies, mystics, businessmen, and priests have special powers which we must realize and put to work; we are the pragmatists who cook rice and make bread, but we are also sensitive to the things which are unseen but real, which nourish the spirit. Take happiness, for example. Does it consist of a pleasant dishwashing machine in our kitchens? Or depend upon a college education? You can count upon your fingers the times when you have been truly happy, usually in retrospect. You recall, 'John and I were happy when we were traveling in Venice'—but actually you spent most of your time there worrying over lost luggage. Gaiety and happiness must not be confused. Jesus was gay at the wedding at Cana, but his real happiness came when he cured

the blind, the lepers, nymphomaniacs, gave a daughter back
to her grieving family. Happiness includes someone other
than yourself. That is why it is important for women to go
on saving in bamboo sticks, clam shells, sugar bags, envelopes,
tiny coins to remind them they are exactly the same as
women in other countries. They need someone who cares.
Even in a Space Age, emotions, hopes cannot be fed into a
machine on a slotted card. No matter how rapidly science
develops computers that can think faster than men, can
machines feel compassion? Women are the stubborn in-
dividualists, the sentimentalists, if you will, but earthy wise
by nature; they consider modern miracles as facts which
God has known all along but which man is just growing
up enough to find out for himself. As a child learns to walk.

"Women even take miracles in their stride, for their own
bodies produce them. They say calmly, 'Artificial insemina-
tion is possible, of course; but can the biochemistry lab put
together the elements of the human body to make a living
baby? Even science admits a child needs more than proper
feeding and dry diapers to develop; he needs *love.*' "

Nor can a machine grind out forgiveness; both come at the
sign of the Cross. During World War Two when the American prisoners at Santo Tomas Prison Camp in Manila (at
the University which is twenty-five years older than Harvard
University) had been nearly starving to death after the
Filipino Christians were no longer allowed to bring them
food, Ruth Harris's job was to pick wild spinach, usually
considered a weed, in a patch behind the camp.

"The weeks turned to months, and the months turned to
years, and Ruth kept the supply of greens coming. Many a
day she wondered if it would be her last in doing the job.
Two things could happen. Either the war would be over or
the enemies would kill them as they did in other places.
Then one day the Allied planes were over Manila. When
Ruth was in the field, she would lie on her back and watch
the B-29s do the bombing formation. She knew exactly what

the next move would be. One day as she watched them she noticed that they were using a different formation. And for a long time no bombs fell. Then she saw what it was. A cross! Salvation would be theirs. The Christians were very positive about it. Early the following morning Allied para-troopers jumped into the compound while the Japanese were bowing to the rising sun. They formed a barricade between the soldiers and the prisoners. An order had been issued to kill the prisoners of war that day." *

The Filipino prisoners had been badly treated after their defeat by the arrogant Japanese militarists, some being kept like animals in caves behind bars in the old Spanish Fort. Yet both American and Filipino Christian women were happy to be members of the First Fellowship of Reconcilia-tion Team that went around the Pacific in 1956. Carmen Armonio, who took Shanti Solomon's place when she was refused admission into Korea, was a mother and a teacher. Her own family and her school had suffered bitterly under the Japanese military, but she showed both Korean and Japanese women how to forgive. Margaret Shannon, Execu-tive secretary of Church Women United, who was also a member of this first group of Christian women out of which grew the Fellowship of the Least Coin, tells what happened:

"As we moved through Korea, we listened to the burden of an oft-repeated prayer—so many families separated by that line which said some were of the North and some of the South. No one blamed them for what they were feeling. But Carmen knew what her testimony must be.

"She did not describe the atrocities which she had seen. She simply said, 'We both have lived under a conquering na-tion, and I want to tell you how hard it was to remember what Jesus said about loving your enemies and forgiving them that persecute you. But after the war, we decided that at six o'clock each night we should pause for a moment

* *Ecumenical Mission,* published by Board of Foreign Missions of the Pres-byterian Church in the U.S.A., 1957.

to pray for the Japanese people. It was then that spiritual
power began to flow back into our lives . . .'

"Because her testimony was genuine, and because it filled
a need, the Koreans listened. On her last day, she listed the
things she liked about their country: the loyal womenfolk
in the churches, the lovely mountains, and the persimmons!

"At the luncheon later which Shanti and the rest of us enjoyed with the church women in Tokyo, the low tables were
beautifully decorated with persimmon leaves. As was their
custom each signed the back of the gay red leaves in much
the same way as our dinner partners sign menus for souve-
nirs. And then we remembered about Carmen and the persimmons and told the women in Tokyo the story of her
testimony on their behalf before the Koreans. Every Christian heart there responded, and immediately another leaf
was signed with Japanese love to be sent to their Filipino
friend who had borne witness to the forgiveness in the heart
of God. We each put our leaf into our Testaments next to
the 22nd Chapter of the Book of Revelation: *On either side
of the river was there the tree of life . . . and the leaves of
the tree were for the healing of the nations . . .*"

The Least Coin Fellowship feels that forgiveness becomes
easier when women meet each other in person, that the
movement to unite all women in prayer and mutual giving
took a great leap forward whenever women of differing cultures and political ideology met *face to face.* The Fellowship therefore sets aside yearly some of the small coins to
insure that such personal encounters shall take place whether
at Mindolo, among Africans of different tribes studying how
to make better homes, or in Anderson, Indiana, where in
the summer of 1967 I was privileged to meet with one hundred Christian leaders from forty-two different countries at
an International Consultation. During this week, we ate,
slept, and talked together, discussing informally our mutual
problems of how to change our adolescents from "rioters"
into responsible citizens, how to meet the frightening lem-

minglike migration of people from country slums into city ghettos, how to substitute Christian tolerance and positive action for wars that try to settle disputes by killing off both sides.

"We must recognize our problems at home as part of the international struggle for racial equality. We could well call ourselves 'a developing country,' " said the one woman from the American Deep South whose home city had recently been partially burned and the business district destroyed by violence. She reported at our group meeting, "I was asked to speak to our Women's Club on the Berlin Wall, but when I got to the hall, I pointed out, 'We have a Berlin Wall right here in our own home town. We live behind a wall of privilege. Are we going to tear it down or ignore it at our peril?' "

"Women alone cannot change the world, but we have done little to foster our own special talents," Lisa Sergio pointed out at Anderson to the listening Africans in their gorgeous long tight gowns and immense bright headdresses; the Indians in saris that flowed behind them like silken water; the dark-haired Indonesians in their gay sarongs; the Americans in miniskirts and more discreet cotton dresses; a very tall Dutch baroness sitting beside a tiny Japanese. They might look exotic to each other, talk different languages, but they all had the same problem of building a Christian home in a chaotic, violent world where moral values were shifting rapidly. Miss Sergio pointed out as Shanti had, "The place to change the world is not on the battlefield but in the home. I believe our job is not to try to outdo men but to supplement them, to restore the spirit by which strong men are made. The real crisis today is not at Vietnam or at Suez, but in the lack of moral values, the decay of the family." Here women must be the G.I.s in the Army of Peace.

Miss Sergio, the daughter of an Italian baron but an American by choice, knows whereof she speaks, for she has lived and worked in many countries. Formerly the first

woman radio commentator in Europe, she now conducts a
weekly Sunday morning broadcast in Washington, D.C.,
called "Prayer Through the Ages." She holds the honorary
degree of Doctor of Human Letters from St. Mary Notre
Dame, the Cross of Chevalier of the Legion of Honor
of France. She believes with Shanti Solomon and Rathie
Selvaratnam, who were in her audience, that international
peace must begin with the individual in her own home. Mrs.
Sergio suggested that Mary had already done an excellent job
of training the boy, Jesus, by the time he was only twelve.

When Mary rebuked her son for worrying his parents by
staying in the temple without permission, she revealed that
she was the discipliner of the child. When Jesus answered
her frankly and without fear, He reflected the intimacy between them. Mary had also taught him to endure slaps, injustice, to think on his own. She had faith in him as a young
man and did not try to "boss" him in public. At the Cana
wedding, she merely asked the servants, "Whatever he says
unto you, do!" Mary did not try to explain the miracle; she
simply believed in her son. In the same way, mother to son
and daughter, even unlettered women who do not understand mathematical formulae nor spaceships, can still ground
their children in the miracle of our common humanity.
What good is traveling to the stars if we cannot manage our
own small planet?

Naturally, at Anderson I joined Shanti Solomon with Rita
Luk and Rayann Ma of Hong Kong and Rathie Selvaratnam
of the Least Coin Fellowship in their discussion group, because by now they were familiar friends.

"But you should be with the American group!" one of the
coordinators urged me. "You don't belong here in Asia!"

"Yes, she does," Shanti smiled, her eyes twinkling at me
under her smooth brown hair, her blue sari a cloud around
her shoulders. "We have just lived together for two days in
Delhi and a week-end in New England."

She had come down from Etawah to Delhi to tell me

about how she had happened to start the Least Coin Fellowship, traveling third class on the train because she did not want to waste money on "luxuries." No one not used to Indian trains can conceive of the sheer physical stamina necessary for the thousands of miles Shanti travels across India as Secretary for Women's Work of the United Church of North India. Trains are slow, hot in summer and icy with their cement floors and no heat in winter. One can buy food through the open windows from hawkers at the stations where the trains often seem to take root, but the toilets are usually filthy, and as one train conductor explained to me once, "coeducational." So are the first-class sleeping apartments for four to six people where the woman traveler has to take her own bedding, and expect that a fellow traveler, often a man, may pre-empt the lower berth unless she gets there first. But Shanti sits up all night in the midst of a smothering crowd, on the wooden seats of the third class, soothing a crying baby so that his mother can snatch a few moments of rest; she rides among old men with their peculiar odor of age and cheap tobacco, among frightened village women who have never traveled by train before so must be soothed when the engine snorts. I could imagine her as a pool of quiet in all this turmoil as she had been in the busy restaurant in Delhi to which she took me to tea because "This was Reuben's favorite place. We always came here together." Since both her and my husband had died during the past few years, we sat there in friendly silence, lost in bittersweet memories, two women who knew what it meant to be loved. Oh yes, we belonged together.

We did not mention the riots in Hong Kong, where Rayann and John Ma, both of whom were contributing much to the consultation at Anderson, had four children living in worrisome danger, nor did we discuss theology. "We Christians from many denominations are much nearer together than we realize when we emphasize the things we have in common rather than those that separate us," Shanti remarked. A letter to her from Vietnam where the refugees are chiefly Buddhist had called the rice sent to Asian relief by the Fellowship of the Least Coin, as "a treasure of love coming to us in the time of our need." "Differences are for theologians to worry about, not us laity." Shanti slid the letter into her bag. "A diversity of ideas is not in reality a barrier but a richness God has given us. Gandhi has said, 'There are so many hungry people that God cannot appear to them except in the form of bread.' Well, we break bread on our communion tables in India." Shanti went on. "Rice is used at the Lord's Table by the aborigines in Sarawak. What matter if the symbols are as different as our Least Coins are?"

The breaking of bread together became for me one of the poignant experiences of my life when we women, two by two, from half a hundred different nations re-enacted the Walk to Emmaus under the tall shade trees of the Anderson campus one summer evening. As Jesus had walked and talked after his resurrection, unrecognized by the worried disciples on their way to Emmaus, we were invited to select a woman from a country other than our own with whom to share our thoughts and experiences. In front of each place at the long table, as a gift, was a crooked piece of unvarnished wood. My partner was Pat Wilson, a bright-haired, vigorous young mother from New Zealand, where she managed a parsonage for her preacher husband. (I understood what a rigorous job that was, for I grew up in a manse.) I had seen Pat only casually to admire her vivacity and laughter; on the surface, we had very little in common. Or so we thought.

"Bob, my husband, and I have four children: Anne, eleven, Ross, nine, Robyn, six, and little John, five," Pat introduced herself and her family as we walked quietly together in the cool of the evening. "We came to this country so Bob could get more theological training to guide our own young New Zealand people who are upset by world violence as are your adolescents here. He was offered a college chaplaincy in

Oregon but on our way driving there, both Bob and Anne became very ill with hepatitis, had to go at once to hospital upon our arrival. They were put into an isolation ward for special care which is very expensive and we had no medical insurance. In our country, like England, we have public health service; a poor preacher certainly could not afford insurance for six!

"You can imagine how alone I felt when that ambulance drove off from the apartment we had just moved into. No money, no one with whom to consult, fear that Bob and Anne might both die. I was too proud to ask any stranger for financial help, but I did find a job selling in a department store, where I had to work late till 8:30 two nights a week. I had never left the children alone in my life, but now Anne, the eldest, was in the hospital, Ross would have to handle the younger children; but he was only nine, the happy-go-lucky of the family who was always making jokes, casual about everything. I worried all the first day, but when I hurried home that night, Ross had bathed and fed the two younger children; they were all in bathrobes, ready to rush into my arms!

"Buying food for that gang at American prices left my pocketbook empty by the end of the first week, but I did not worry, since tomorrow was pay day. But I was told at the office, 'It is our policy to pay only at the end of the second week; then when you leave us, you will have accumulated two weeks' severance pay.' I stared at the clerk, horrified. I needed that money *now!* I sleepwalked up the long hill back to the apartment, wondering how I was going to tell the children there would be nothing to eat tomorrow. I was so tired I told them exactly what had happened.

" 'Don't worry. We'll pray,' Ross said easily.

"They'd been trained not to be afraid, that God was always with them. What could I say? He made me feel so much better that I opened my mail from home and out dropped a check for $14! A neighbor had written, 'I thought, being in a strange country and all, you might like to buy something special for the children for Christmas . . .' We ate for the next week on that $14; then Anne and Bob came home, well, from the hospital. Why couldn't I have as much faith as my own children?" Pat smiled but there were tears in her eyes as our clasped hands swung between us as we walked together. Had the disciples held hands on the way to Emmaus? Many Oriental men do, happily, without embarrassment.

"Almost the same thing happened to me," I told Pat. "Only the strange country I was in was Spain, where my sick husband was recuperating. One morning we suddenly realized that we didn't have enough money left to pay our fare home! I prayed for guidance but I couldn't stop worrying. Then I, too, opened my mail to find the offer of a job in Michigan; a check for $500 was enclosed in the envelope! My new boss had written, 'I just had a feeling that, with a sick husband, maybe you could use this advance.' " As Pat from New Zealand and I from New England on the strange path in Indiana, stared at each other, I added, "I guess on both letters, angels licked the postage stamps!"

Silently she held out the crooked piece of unvarnished wood in her hand and it fitted into mine—to make a Cross.

Pink and blue blobs on the map merged into a friendly world at Anderson as we Americans got acquainted with a Bantu nurse from Africa, a Quaker from Kenya, the head of a maternity center from Nigeria, a colonel in the Salvation Army from England, a teacher from Malaya, a faculty member from Jan Hus Seminary in Czechoslovakia, one of the oldest theological schools in the world, dating back to the Protestant Reformation. Mrs. Martin Luther King, whose nonviolent work among American Negroes had been helped by the Fellowship of the Least Coin, led our evening song service as the shadows crept down from the trees onto the lawn. It was no accident that the favorite song which you heard hummed on the sidewalk, in the dormitory corridors

and the last thing before you went to sleep at night was
African, *Kum Ba Yah*. Translated, it means *Come By Here*.
The haunting refrain went:

> Someone's crying, Lord, Kum Ba Yah,
> Someone's singing, Lord, Kum Ba Yah,
> Someone's praying, Lord, Kum Ba Yah . . .

Iron and bamboo curtains, differences between yellow,
black, brown or white faces simply did not exist when you
drank your breakfast coffee with a Chinese and a Yugoslavian
preacher's wife led your Bible study group every morning.
Her husband had been holding services in their Reformed
Protestant Church in Rumenka for thirty years. Under the
Communist regime, preachers were few, she explained, so
the laity had had to take over many parishes. But was that
not perhaps a good thing? The early church had considered
every Christian layman and woman as a priest. In 1966 when
Dorothy Wagner, Secretary for Women's Relations of the
United Presbyterian Church, was visiting in Rumenka, she
spoke of the Fellowship of the Least Coin. Immediately one
parishioner rushed to find a matchbox and held it out triumphantly. It was already full of saved dinars!

"Many of us still use oil lamps so the matchboxes are
convenient," the minister's wife explained at Anderson. "We
now have seventy Least Coin members in our group. Many
more women who have small children and cannot come to
our meetings fill their matchboxes at home. Since we are
not allowed to send money out of the country, the amount
we raise is credited to our account in Geneva and sent on in
the currency of whatever country it helps.

"Our main job as Christian women in a political regime
such as ours is to prove that love can be a positive way of
life more satisfying than hate. When trouble comes to our
women, when perhaps some of the family are sent to prison,
they need not only comforting but to find out that forgive-

ness helps *you* as much as the one who has injured you."
She sighed. "Hate is a sickness and forgiveness a hard lesson
you have to keep relearning. But even a few dinars given in
the name of Christ is different from merely human compassion because it gives both giver and recipient someone
bigger than they are to hold onto."

She went on quietly, this gentle fearless woman who was
keeping alight a little candle in a windy world, "When my
son was small, in the fourth grade at school he rushed into
my kitchen one afternoon and burst into tears. 'I hate history,' he sobbed. 'It is nothing but fights and killing other
people!'

"Our job as women is to show love can write a new history
of its own. In our country Christians are respected if we do
not pretend to be what we are not, if we are good doctors,
good teachers, good neighbors. Even where the state has
taken over public welfare, social service, we can work with
them to put *heart* into our giving as the Fellowship of the
Least Coins does."

This slender Yugoslavian with the worn lovely face looked
at me consideringly, then ventured, "Sometimes you Americans seem to have a deep loneliness, a fear that you are liked
for what you have, not what you are. Christians should have
a hidden joy that does not need gratitude, for they themselves have received so much."

Whether they collect their tiny coins in clam shells as does
one group of women on Cape Cod, Massachusetts, or in little
toy houses as the women do in Guatemalan churches, in a
plastic cowboy boot in Venezuela, or in toy birds or hens
made of clay in Colombia, the Least Coin Fellowship is finding that tolerance is infectious. Today Roman Catholics and
Protestants in Colombia are cooperating, often for the first
time, to eradicate illiteracy. One of Colombia's biggest problems has been education, since 45 percent of the people cannot read or write and in the countryside the percentage of
literacy may go as low as 25 percent. So it was a real tragedy

when in 1948 the ruling dictatorship shut down, destroyed, or confiscated many Protestant schools. When in 1962 under a more democratic government this ban was lifted, the Least Coin Fellowship promptly sent help to rebuild and reopen such schools. The townspeople, eager for their sons and daughters to learn to read and write, gladly gave their hand labor and transported materials, zinc for roofing and cement for walls and floors "from the place where the road ends to the final destination, sometimes two days on horseback, crossing rivers and mountains."

"Most of these schools have by now returned to a convalescent life," reported one teacher at Anderson who travels around the country as supervisor of rural education. "The social and religious antagonism which has been our problem rather than racial discrimination has been mellowing. Recently, when I invited high society Roman Catholic women to a tea, I was warned they would not come—but they did. What's more, they asked me back to meet one of their own groups. In one village where I hoped to start classes, I decided to consult first with the priest who is always the arbitrator of the community. 'But you are a Protestant. He will not even speak with you!' I was warned by anxious villagers. But I went to his rectory just the same, where he received me graciously. Why not, when we were both interested in the same things, boiling the water to prevent disease, child welfare, educating the children of his fold?" She laughed. "I even introduced the Presbyterian missionaries to their neighbor, the good priest!"

These concerned women who would go home from Anderson to political unrest in Hong Kong, Indonesia, Singapore, to civil war in Nigeria, to racial violence in the USA were reminded that they should not be discouraged but be thankful for this growing tolerance among Christians. The Anderson ecumenical group were urged: "Let us thank God for these stars in the darkness around us and that we walk under those stars."

Another such "star" appeared in the Christian firmament recently when Church Women United, which reaches nearly seventeen million women around the world (chiefly Protestant but more recently including also Roman Catholics), "accepted gladly" the invitation to help sponsor the Fellowship of the Least Coin. Women of a few denominations in the United States had participated from the beginning of the Fellowship; now in 1967 Church Women United agreed to become a further channel of participation for others. Esther Bautista, the Fellowship's secretary, came from Manila to offer a personal invitation to the Board of Managers to cooperate, a decision ratified a few months later by two thousand delegates gathered at Purdue University from more than fifty countries. This was fitting since both organizations believe that the power of prayer is essential for building a "peaceable kingdom" and also because Margaret Shannon, executive secretary for Church Women United, had also been one of the 1956 Fellowship Team of Reconciliation whose Indian member, Shanti Solomon, had first envisioned the Fellowship of the Least Coin.

Rathie Selvaratnam, chairman of the Central Committee in Asia who decides where the Least Coins from six continents shall be allocated, was asked to write the 1968 program for The World Day of Prayer. This very special annual petition by all Christian women for the help of Almighty God was initiated in the United States and is now further sponsored by indigenous church women in one hundred and twenty-seven countries. The Circle of Praying Hands designed by Rayann Ma might well serve as insignia for both women's organizations, for it is the mother's job to build character in her family as well as healthy bodies; it is at her knee that the child's first prayer is said.

> "For so the whole round earth is every way
> Bound by gold chains about the feet of God."

Mrs. Dorothy Nichols Dolbey, the newly elected president of Church Women United, former mayor of Cincinnati and recipient of the Mary Margaret McBride Citizenship Citation as well as the Brotherhood Citation of the National Council of Christians and Jews, finds today's world turmoil a challenge to women to put to work their special genius as guardians of the individual, to see to it that recipients of relief, both locally and internationally, be treated as people rather than as "cases."

"A turbulent time of change can also be a time of opportunity to grow in knowledge and understanding," she pointed out to the listening women gathered in Indiana not only from the United States but from the far corners of the earth.

"The population explosion, urbanization, the rebellion of youth, the frustrations of an individual in a technological society—all of these are causes and results of our constantly changing world."

"Far too often individuals are looked through and over," she stressed. "This is what the American Negro is saying, this is what our discontented youth are saying—please, look at us as human beings—you don't even know that we are here—look at all the people at home and abroad as persons, as human beings with the same fears, tears, the same hopes. Color, nationality, continents melt away, disappear."

From the opposite side of the world, an Asian member of the Fellowship of the Least Coin has given a similar clear call to action. In the *Circle of Prayer,* a collection assembled by the women of Hong Kong of "thoughts and prayers to be used when making the offering of the Least Coin," Ranee Maliezer of Malaysia says:

"The rise and fall of great nations has depended not so much on kings and battles as the history books assume, but on the status of the women. Where and when they have been regarded as 'the Devi,' or the loving spirit of the home and the eyes of the nation, countries have reached great peaks of achievement and civilization. Where women have been regarded as chattels and playthings without souls; where the attitude has prevailed that it is better to be yoked to a tiger than to a woman; or that heaven is a place full of dancing girls; or, that heaven, thank God, is a place where there are no women; where women have been treated as second-class citizens—there once powerful nations have crumbled into the dust of oblivion.

"The well-being of the home, the state and the community is in the hands of its women. Where they are active, well-informed, concerned about the needs of the community and willing to give generously of their time, talents, and titles, all is well. Where they are constantly fretting, fuming, rushing, domineering, intolerant, lashing themselves into importance, power, and prestige, all human institutions peter out and die a natural death.

"We are the nation builders of the world, queens on our thrones. Our life is indeed a many-splendored thing. It is we who know the miracle of loving and being loved. The wonders of the modern world have been laid at our feet, giving us time to live, to work and to be quiet. Our boundaries of love and service have extended beyond our homes into the cities, the slums and the outlying villages. The whole world has become our parish. We have become the eyes of the world."

She ended, "O God, make us aware of our many-splendored lives and our responsibilities—in our homes and in the eyes of the nation. Remind us that we can no longer live on our individual islands, that we cannot live alone, and that we, all, belong to the same world."

Rathie Selvaratnam put it more simply when she advised not only the Fellowship of the Least Coin but God-fearing women everywhere, " 'Bear ye one another's burdens and so fulfill the law of Christ.' "

INDEX

A Note About the Author

Grace Nies Fletcher was born in Townsend, Massachusetts. She graduated Phi Beta Kappa from Boston University and later studied at Columbia and Ohio Wesleyan. Mrs. Fletcher has traveled widely in Europe and the Far East, as well as in America. To gather material for IN QUEST OF THE LEAST COIN, she visited Kenya, India, Indonesia, Vietnam, Thailand, The Philippines, Hong Kong, Ceylon, and Japan. On previous trips, she has lectured for university courses in creative writing and for women's organizations in both this country and in Japan. Her articles have appeared in a number of popular magazines, notably the *Saturday Evening Post, Ladies' Home Journal, McCall's,* and the *Reader's Digest.* Previous books include *What's Right With Our Young People, The Fabulous Flemings of Kathmandu, The Whole World's in His Hand,* and *I Was Born Tomorrow.* The author, who is a widow, is the mother of a grown son.

1968

Date Due

Code 436-279, CLS-4, Broadman Supplies, Nashville, Tenn.,
Printed in U.S.A.